ONE RED PAPERCLIP

How a small piece of stationery turned into a great big adventure

KYLE MACDONALD

EBURY PRESS

3 5 7 9 10 8 6 4

First published in 2007 by Ebury Press, an imprint of Ebury Publishing
A Random House Group Company

The Random House Group Limited Reg. No. 954009

Addresses for companies within the Random House Group
can be found at www.randomhouse.co.uk

A CIP catalogue record for this book is available from the British Library

Designed and typeset by seagulls.net

Printed in the UK by CPI Mackays, Chatham, ME5 8TD

ISBN 9780091914523

For mom and dad and everyone
who made you who you are.

If you can keep your head when all about you
Are losing theirs and blaming it on you,
If you can trust yourself when all men doubt you,
But make allowance for their doubting too;
If you can wait and not be tired by waiting,
Or being lied about, don't deal in lies,
Or being hated, don't give way to hating,
And yet don't look too good, nor talk too wise:

If you can dream – and not make dreams your master,
If you can think – and not make thoughts your aim;
If you can meet with Triumph and Disaster
And treat those two impostors just the same;
If you can bear to hear the truth you've spoken
Twisted by knaves to make a trap for fools,
Or watch the things you gave your life to, broken,
And stoop and build 'em up with worn-out tools:

If you can make one heap of all your winnings
And risk it all on one turn of pitch-and-toss,
And lose, and start again at your beginnings
And never breathe a word about your loss;
If you can force your heart and nerve and sinew
To serve your turn long after they are gone,
And so hold on when there is nothing in you
Except the Will which says to them: "Hold on!"

If you can talk with crowds and keep your virtue,
Or walk with kings – nor lose the common touch,
If neither foes nor loving friends can hurt you,
If all men count with you, but none too much;
If you can fill the unforgiving minute
With sixty seconds' worth of distance run,
Yours is the Earth and everything that's in it,
And – which is more – you'll be a Man, my son!

Rudyard Kipling (1865–1936)

Dom and I round the corner.

People are everywhere.

Hundreds.

The whole town.

Literally.

We walk to the front of the crowd and see Bert and Pat.

We shake their hands.

I wave shyly to the crowd and the ceremony begins.

We stand for the national anthem.

Mom and Dad are right behind us.

Speeches are made, formal introductions take place.

Pat, the mayor, raises a piece of paper in the air.

"Here in my right hand is the deed to the house behind us. It is my honour to hereby ask Kyle MacDonald to step forward with his trade item and sign this piece of paper to make the trade official."

The crowd claps. I step forward, and a hush falls over the crowd.

I smile and hand over my trade item.

Pat hands me a pen.

I sign the deed.

We smile.

Pat says, "To make this official, it must be witnessed. Gord?"

Gord, the Mountie, steps forward and signs the deed.
Pat says, "Welcome to Kipling."
We cut a red ribbon with a pair of scissors.
Dom and I hold hands and walk up the stairs.
I reach out and open the front door.
I face the crowd to speak.
My lip starts to tremble.
It is so real.
So perfect.
So silent.
Dom holds my hand.
We say thank you.
We wave to the crowd.
And walk through the door.
Into the future.

one red paperclip

It was the best idea ever. Bigger and Better. It had *legs.* Bigger and Better was a game. A mash-up between a scavenger hunt and trick-or-treating. You'd start with a small object and go door to door to see if anybody would trade something bigger and better for it. When you made a trade you'd go to another door and see if you could trade your new object for something bigger and better. Eventually, with enough hard work, you could end up with something much bigger and better than you started with.

For example, you could start with a spoon. You'd take that spoon to the neighbour's house, and maybe they'd offer you a boot. You could then take the boot to the next neighbour and they'd say, "Hey! I could use a boot, I accidentally threw one of mine out the passenger window onto the shoulder of the freeway last week. I have an old microwave. Would you like to trade that boot for a microwave?"

At this point you'd nod yes, take the microwave and run as fast as possible to find your friends and show off your new microwave. You'd have a great story about how you got your microwave and from that moment on stare at every solitary boot on the side of a freeway and wonder if that was *the* boot. Then a few weeks later your mom would come into your room and say, "Hey, I can't find my antique spoon. Have you seen it anywhere?" At this point you'd shake your head no and she'd say,

"And do you know anything about that smelly old microwave in the garage?"

Bigger and Better was awesome.

I grew up in Port Moody, a suburb east of Vancouver, Canada. Friends at high school told tales of amazing Bigger and Better adventures. One group started with a penny and traded up to a couch in just one afternoon. Another group started with a clothespeg and worked their way up to a fridge in an evening. Rumour had it that in the next suburb over, some kids started early in the morning with a toothpick and traded all the way up to a car before the day was over. A *car*. Of course nobody had proof that any of these things actually happened, but it didn't matter. Suburban legend or not, it was possible. *Anything* was possible. And we were all about making anything possible.

We were sixteen. We'd just passed our road tests. The driver's licences were just itching to be used. There was only one thing on our mind: cars. We wanted to be Marty McFly. We wanted to park our freshly waxed black 1985 Toyota pickup on an angle in the garage and turn the front wheels to enhance its sportiness. We wanted to take Jennifer up to the lake for the big party on the weekend. Yeah, where we were going, we wouldn't need roads. So much was possible. Our children could one day meet a middle-aged DeLorean-driving mad scientist who would invent the flux capacitor and accidentally get sent back in time to right all the wrong choices we'd made in our life so we could then realize our dream of being science fiction writers.

It was possible.

But we were sixteen. And never read science-fiction books. Or even remotely considered the idea of being *writers*.

We looked at each other and nodded. That night was the

night. It was going to happen. We were going to do it. We were going to play Bigger and Better until we got cars. Tonight. All we needed was a toothpick. We couldn't find a toothpick, so we "found" the next best thing: a Christmas tree from the local Christmas tree lot.

We picked up the Christmas tree and carried it over to the first house that still had their lights on. We knocked on the door. We heard footsteps. We looked at one another. We were *so* getting cars. A shadow approached the door and reached for the handle. Cars by the end of the night. The door opened. A man stepped into the door frame, looked at us with the Christmas tree in our hands, made a slight face, and said, "Yes?" We quickly explained how we were playing Bigger and Better, told him our plan to trade up to a car by the end of night, and waited in full expectation. All he had to do was trade us something. Anything. He looked at the Christmas tree, laughed slightly, and said, "Sorry, guys, I'd love to help you out, but I don't have a use for a second Christmas tree." He stretched his arm towards the front room and pointed at the most over-elaborately decorated Christmas tree of all time. It shone bright white. It was like heaven, in Christmas tree form. We looked back at our meagre little tree, hung our heads low, and watched the car in our minds go *poof.* He shrugged his shoulders, smiled, and said, "Maybe try next door? Good luck!"

We walked off and looked at the tree. It was too late at night to play Bigger and Better. We'd try next door tomorrow. Yeah, tomorrow had next door written all over it. Tomorrow had "car" written all over it.

But we never played Bigger and Better tomorrow.

We quit because Bigger and Better wasn't as easy as we expected it to be.

That was ten years ago. *Ten years* had passed since that night we'd played Bigger and Better. So many things had happened since then. I'd finished school, travelled, met new people, worked all over the world, and experienced so many things. I even shook Al Roker's hand. In all those years I never finished that game of Bigger and Better. But it was still the best idea ever.

I looked out into the distance and imagined the possibilities. A car from a toothpick. It was possible. But how would I trade a toothpick for a car nowadays? I made a confident face, and looked even further into the distance, as though it would help. It might have made for an amazing inspiration-seeking moment in a movie, except the distance wasn't a setting sun smouldering over the remains of a freshly annihilated evil alien civilization or a windswept seashore with waves and unsurpassed vistas. The distance was a brick wall five feet from my head. A brick wall that held up one side of the small one-bedroom apartment in Montreal that my girlfriend Dominique and I rented.

I'd moved to Montreal with Dom the previous summer after she got a job as a fight attendant with an airline that had since gone bankrupt. She'd found a job at a hospital as a dietician soon after that. We'd been together for three years. While I looked into the distance and reminisced about juvenile adventures of yore, Dom was working. Dom had a job. I was "between jobs". I'd been "between jobs" for almost a year now, bridging the gap from time to time by working at trade shows promoting products for friends.

But those trade shows were few and far between.

I was just some guy. What was I thinking? I'd just stared at a brick wall for the better part of an hour. I'd nearly *wasted* an entire afternoon. I remembered the job at hand. My résumé. My cover letter. My future. That whole get-a-job thing.

Rent was due soon, and I couldn't sponge off Dom for another month. I'd sponged for a few months. It had to stop. It was my turn to provide. I looked at the résumé on my computer screen. Motivational words from my high school business education teacher rang out in my mind. She'd say, "You need to sell yourself to a potential employer. You need to showcase your skills." She'd then pull out an overhead projector slide and show us how to implement the five secrets of the perfect résumé. And boy did those five secrets work! We all had jobs at fast food joints in less than a week. Ten years ago, a bagful of free burgers pretty much guaranteed you were on easy street. Living at home makes everything so much simpler.

Dom was about to cut me off if I didn't get my act together. I had to figure something out. Fast. I asked myself a simple question: "Did I *really* want to implement the five secrets of the perfect résumé or did I want to do something else?" Something else sounded pretty good right now. I didn't want to sell myself to anyone. I just wanted to do *things*. I wanted to *explore*. I wanted to *play*. I wanted to *be*.

But things were different now. I wasn't some punk kid who "borrowed" Christmas trees and lived with his parents. I was an unemployed twenty-five-year-old guy lucky enough to have a girlfriend who helped cover my portion of the rent while I was "between jobs".

I was sick of sponging off others. I was sick of being "between jobs". I was tired of quotation-mark-accompanied euphemisms for being unemployed. There was really only one thing I wanted to do. I wanted to *provide*. I wanted to put food on the table. I wanted to break the cycle we were in. We worked hard for our money, then shovelled it directly into the landlord's pocket. Well, *Dom* worked hard for our money, but I definitely helped shovel it into the landlord's pocket. Sure, paying rent's not all bad. There's something to be said for being able to covertly pack up all your stuff in the middle of the night, then fly away to another country on a moment's notice. Don't get me wrong, landlords are often pleasant, trustworthy folk. I just didn't want anything to do with them. A place where you pay rent is just somewhere you haven't moved out of yet. But with enough time, care, and effort, a place of your own can become a home.

I wanted to come home at the end of the day, hang my top hat on the hat stand by the doorway, look up at the roof above my head, and smile with satisfaction that I owned that roof. A roof of our own. We could do anything under that roof. If we wanted to knock down a wall, then that's exactly what we could do. Nobody could say otherwise.

If I started small, thought big, and had fun, it could all happen.

It was possible.

For it to be possible, I had to start. I had to do more than the first time I'd tried to play Bigger and Better. The time I'd never even made a single trade. Bigger and Better had just stared back at me for the last decade. Laughing at me. Cackling, even. I thought about it again. It would take a few weeks to get a job, but I could walk outside and make Bigger and Better happen *now*. I made up my mind then and there. *Now* was the time. Not only would I play Bigger and Better, I would play it *well*. I would become the greatest Bigger and Better player the world had ever seen, *bar none*. Or I had just come up with the most elaborate way to put off getting a job. Ever. Either way, I had to give it a shot. I squinted and lowered my head slightly. The résumé and cover letter could wait. I had a score to settle with Bigger and Better.

If I was going to make it happen, I needed an object to start with. Something less Christmas treeish than a Christmas tree. And something not blatantly stolen.

I looked down at the desk. It was a mess. Things strewn everywhere. A pen. A roll of tape. Way too many cables. A stapler. Computer speakers. My résumé and cover letter. An unmailed letter. A postcard. A banana peel. A framed picture of an eagle in flight. Various cereal bowls in various stages of not being washed. I looked back at the draft copy of my résumé and cover letter. Two sheets of paper held together by a red paperclip.

One red paperclip.

I unclipped the red paperclip from the papers and held it up to my eye.

It was perfect.

This was it.

All I had to do was go outside and trade with somebody. Surely *somebody* would have something bigger and better than one red paperclip. This was it. I was going to do it. Bigger and Better was going to get *served*.

I put the red paperclip on the desk and took a picture of it. I walked to the door and pulled the handle. The door swung open. I lifted my right foot into the air. As my right foot came forward to the threshold of the door frame, the phone rang. My foot hung in the air, just short of the outside hallway. The phone rang again. I spun around, almost in slow motion. I slowly slunk away from the door and lifted the phone from the receiver.

"Hello?" I said.

"Hey."

It was Dom.

"What are you doing?" she said.

"Not much," I said.

"Did you finish your résumé?" she asked.

"Not yet. I'm just taking a break."

"Right. *A break*. How long have you been working on that thing?"

I felt guilty. Dom was so good to me. She'd covered my rent for months. She could've kicked me out into the street. Heck, *I* would've kicked me out into the street. I owed her. We chatted a while and made plans for dinner.

I walked back to the computer and shoved the red paperclip in my wallet. What was I thinking anyhow? Bigger and Better? Settling scores? With a kids' game? I shook my head and turned on my computer. Maybe I'd play Bigger and Better another day. After I had a job, enough money to cover the rent, and a day off. Then I could play Bigger and Better.

The computer monitor came to life and I got back to my résumé. Over the next three days I hammered out a respectable enough one and halfheartedly emailed it in response to a few job postings on some websites. I also emailed the picture of the red paperclip to myself, as a reminder of something fun I could do once I had a job, and a day off.

Tomorrow came and went many times. The more I thought of my potential new job, the less I thought about my score with Bigger and Better. In my wallet, the red paperclip became buried among my cards, receipts and old coins. I eventually got some calls from people who wanted to interview me for various jobs. Nothing spectacular, but decent enough jobs. I was just thankful that somebody had responded. I went to several interviews but never put my heart into it. I was just "going through the motions" as Mom would have said. Was it because I was a lazy schmo or was it was because the jobs didn't feel right? I couldn't decide. I didn't want to settle for something I wasn't happy with.

I wanted to put my heart into something. I didn't want to *survive*, I wanted to *thrive*. I was running on empty but didn't want to make the move that would fill the tank.

A few weeks later Dom and I flew across the country to Vancouver, on the west coast of Canada, to visit my family. Well, actually, the plane flew across the country, we just sat in our seats. After we'd been in Vancouver a week, Mom and Dom had a "girls' night out", so Dad and I went over to my cousin Ty's place. During a lull in the conversation, I decided to clean out my wallet. I dumped the contents of my wallet on the coffee table.

And out spilled the red paperclip.

I thought again about the idea to trade up from the red paperclip. But this time was different. This time I opened my mouth: "Hey, what do you guys think of this idea?"

I filled them in on Bigger and Better. They thought about it.

"I like it," Dad said.

"I like it too," said Ty.

"Why did you choose a red paperclip?" Dad said.

"It was the first thing I saw," I said.

"When are you going to trade it?" Ty said.

"Well, I need to set some things up before I can start."

"Like what?" Dad said.

"I'll need to get some money first, so I have time to make trades. I should probably set up a website and take a better picture of the paperclip, you know?" I said and looked at my dad.

"Why?" he said.

He had a point. Why did I have to set things up? I just wanted to trade my red paperclip with somebody.

I looked at the paperclip. It was a big "if". Watching as I stared at the paperclip, Dad smirked. He then uttered his favourite secondhand inspirational slogan: "What would you do if you weren't afraid?" he said.

I suddenly had an inexplicable craving for cheese. I thought to myself, *what would I do if I weren't afraid? Also, should I tell Pops that he's a total cheeseball?*

I said, "If I weren't afraid, I'd trade this red paperclip for something."

He smiled and said, "So why don't you?"

I knew I could walk out into the street and ask the first person who came along if they wanted to trade something for my red paperclip, but that just didn't feel right.

"I don't want to pester people, get up in their grill, you know?" It didn't feel right to go around hassling people. There had to be another way.

I said, "You know what would be cool? If people contacted me if *they* wanted to make a trade." I thought about the man with the angelic Christmas tree that we'd bothered with our raggedy old stolen tree. "Instead of bothering people I wish that people who want to trade could get in touch with me."

Ty put his arms up in the air to suggest he'd just realized something extraordinary that was right in front of us all along, and said, "Craigslist! Have you tried putting it on Craigslist? *Everyone* uses Craigslist."

"Can you trade stuff on Craigslist?" I asked.

Ty shook his head in semi-mock disbelief. *Can you trade stuff on Craigslist?*

As we walked over to the computer I looked up at the calendar on the wall.

It was July 12.

Ty brought up the Craigslist site for Vancouver. I found a section marked "barter". Under "Posting Title", I entered: one red paperclip.

I uploaded a picture of the red paperclip I'd sent myself in an email. Under the "Posting Description", I entered the following:

This might not surprise you, but this is a picture of a paperclip. It is red. This red paperclip is currently sitting on my desk next to my computer. I want to trade this paperclip with you for something bigger or better, maybe a pen, a spoon, or perhaps a boot. If you promise to make the trade I will come and visit you, wherever you are, to trade. So, if you have something bigger or better than a red paperclip, email me at biggerorbetter@gmail.com!
Hope to trade with you soon!
Kyle

PS I'm going to make a continuous chain of "up trades" until I get a house. Or an island. Or a house on an island. You get the idea.

I clicked "Publish", and made my intentions public. Sure, my "if you post it, they will come" tactic was pretty optimistic and lazy, but it was better than nothing. I was just trying to trade a silly little red paperclip for something bigger and better. We waited a few minutes, then refreshed my email. Nothing. We waited a few more. Nothing. I started to get antsy. I found the Craigslist sites for a few cities near or not so near Vancouver and Montreal and added a listing for the red paperclip to those. We waited a few more minutes and I clicked on "Refresh". A number of offers were already in my email inbox!

*****I've got a black spork to trade. I love red paperclips.

*****I have a broken #2 pencil to trade for the paper clip!

*****I have a blue felt tip pen, but I am worried that this would not be an even trade due to the slight bend in the side. LOL. Any how if you are serious I would gladly trade my blue pen. I am in Woodbridge, you would have to come out! Thank you!
Bethany

*****Kyle,
I imagine you are wanting to see how far you can take this so I will trade with you a stepometer that I think came from a McDonalds meal deal (I don't eat McDonalds anymore). It is orange and dark gray and has a clock with alarm. I believe it is bigger and better than a paperclip. If you are interested in trading email me back and I will give you directions!
Jacky

Since I'd posted ads in a number of different Craigslist cities I had no idea where each offer had come from. (Posting ads in multiple cities on Craigslist is a big no-no, I later found out. Apparently it's called "spamming" or something like that. I emailed everyone back and asked where each person was located. I added Mom and Dad's phone number and urged people to call if they were in Vancouver. It was sort of important, as I wanted to make the trade in person. And soon. If I was going to do this, *now* was the time. Now is always a great time to do things. I just had to start. If I never started, it would never happen.

I stuffed the miscellany back in my wallet, and Dad and I headed back home. By the time we got there, several more offers were in my inbox:

*****Hi ... We have a fish pen that actually moves like a fish ... back and forth ... rather amusing ... and pretty sweet ... you down? Let us know.
Corinna

*****I happen to have an empty bottle of Wite-Out ... What do you think? Going fast, don't linger.
Chris

*****Dear sir/madam,
I just saw the advert of your (ADS), which you have for sale and I decided to mail you and find out if it is still for sale. I would like to know the present condition and your last offer price with a photo. Thanks as I await to hear from you soon.
Sincerely Cusin Malone

*****My lovely powder blue paper clip for your red one!! I absolutely adore red, it is my favourite colour, and the red paper clip is calling my name, would you trade for that? I could throw in a wonderful new pencil top eraser as well, just so long as I get the fabulous red paper clip!!
Ciao, June

*****I will trade you for a sky blue crayola coloured pencil ... it has been used.
Raine

*****I'll trade you your paper clip for a pair of women's boots. I'm a guy and I don't wear women's boots, but I do use paper and therefore I could use a paper clip.

*******I have a pen, pencil, crayon, envelope or a small box of bandages. Want to trade??**

*******If you are a female and would like to meet for a coffee i will trade you a coffee date for the paper clip and if things work out who knows. Cheers.**
Cezaro

A bunch of family came over to my parents' house the following night. Ricky, the husband of my cousin Carmen, came up to me and said, "Hey, kid, I got you a present." He handed me a box of Wheaties, without a doubt my favourite breakfast cereal with pictures of real life sports heroes on it.

"A box of Wheaties, Ricky? You shouldn't have!" I said.

"Just open the damn box. You know it ain't Wheaties. I figured since you got me a shirt for Christmas, I'd return the favour," he said.

My brother, Scott, and I gave Ricky a Democrat shirt for Christmas, and Ty, a Republican one. They both put them on immediately. Nothing like Christmastime T-shirt politics to get a party started. Nothing. I tore open the Wheaties box and found a short-sleeve button-up work shirt. It was baby blue with pink pinstripes. I turned it over. Above the left breast pocket was a patch with the name "Ricky" in a stylish "patch" font. Another patch was above the right breast pocket. It read "Cintas – 'The Uniform People'".

"Gee Ricky, your old work shirt." I looked up at Ricky and said, matter-of-factly, "You shouldn't have."

He smiled, patted me on the back and said, "Don't mention it, kid!"

I slid the shirt over my T-shirt to show I wasn't going to be "had" and said, "Don't worry, I won't."

When everyone left just before midnight, I checked my email. The offers were continuing to roll in: pencils, crayons, keys, coffee dates, business enquiries from people who addressed me as "sir/madam", and the like. One trader was in Vancouver:

From: Corinna
Hey ... We are in Vancouver ... near Commercial. Now, I hope you understand that this pen is very special. It is wood, and actually moves like a fish!! ... It is very multicoloured, green, blue and red. You let us know when you want to make the trade, and it will be done! Normally we would not trade a simple paperclip for such a wonderful pen ... but it needs to swim other waters ... and I suppose paperclips, can be quite useful. We are, Corinna and Rhawnie. Talk soon ... Later ...
Post-script ... and who are you ... other than "kyle", and where are you??

The phone rang. It was late. I didn't want Mom and Dad to wake up. I ran to the phone. I pushed "talk" before the second ring.

"Hello?" I said.

"Um, hey ... is this Kyle?" There was muffled laughter in the background.

"Yep, that's me."

"My name's Rhawnie." There was a smile in her voice. "My friend Corinna and I, um, we saw your red paperclip on Craigslist and we want to trade with you."

"Cool! What do you guys have?"

"A pen shaped like a fish. Corinna sent you an email."

"Right!" I said. "The fish pen!"

"It's really cool," said Rhawnie.

"I'll bet," I said. "Hey, I'm leaving town tomorrow around noon. Any chance we can meet up before then to make the trade?"

"Sure, but I leave for work early," Rhawnie said.

"What time?"

"I get up around seven and am on my way to work by eight."

"Wanna meet up just before eight?" I said.

"Can we meet somewhere near our place?" she said.

"Yeah, probably. Where do you guys live?"

"Near Commercial," she said.

"Perfect, I'll be driving right past there tomorrow morning anyhow," I said "What works for you?"

"Do you know the 7-Eleven at the corner of First and Nanaimo?" she said.

"Yep" I said.

"How about quarter to eight in front of 7-Eleven?"

"Done. See you then," I said.

"Yep, see you tomorrow."

Click.

It was settled. Tomorrow was the day. I looked up at the clock. It was 12:03 a.m. Tomorrow was already here.

What's your paperclip?

What will you "trade" to make it happen? What's your first move? It doesn't have to be big. Maybe it's just a phone call, or maybe you'll finally ask the question you've wondered about for so long. A red paperclip for a pen shaped like a fish isn't exactly a big commitment. But it's a start.

If you don't start, then how can you finish?

It's pretty simple. If you never start, it won't happen. Every great journey starts with a single step. Just get a foot through the door and make your move. Right foot or left foot, it's your choice.

Start small, think big, and have fun.

If it works small, it might work big, but if you have fun along the way it shouldn't matter either way.

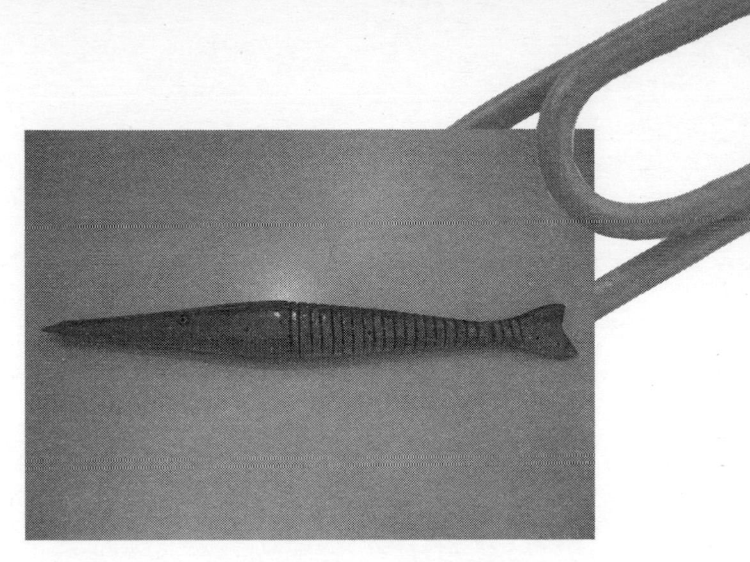

one fish pen

I'd only talked with Rhawnie and Corinna via email and phone, so I had no idea what they looked like. I figured I could find them easily enough. There's really no reason to go to 7-Eleven before noon unless you stop there in a cab at the tail end of a bender to satisfy your craving for microwaveable hamburgers. There are a lot of things that, depending on your level of alcohol intake, go from being the worst idea ever to the best idea ever, and sev burgers are right near the top of that list.

Mom and Dom came along for the ride. I pulled the van into the parking lot. A few cars, but nothing else. I immediately thought I'd been the victim of a Craigslist-instigated prank. *As if* two women were going to show up that early to trade a fish-shaped pen for a red paperclip with a guy they'd met on the Internet. *As if.* I bit my lip. When you've been "had", you don't want to let it get to you. You just roll with the punches and act like nothing's out of the ordinary.

We passed a parked car and turned into a parking spot. As we pulled in we saw two women sitting on the curb in front of the store. They didn't have microwaveable hamburgers in their hands. I felt relieved – not for their lack of sev burgers but because it meant I probably wasn't being stood up from a Craigslist posting.

Mom looked over at the two women and laughed, "That looks like them! Do you have your red paperclip?"

I rolled my eyes and said, "Yes, *Mom.*"

I tapped Ricky's shirt pocket to double check. It was there. Not that I didn't already know that. I lifted the gear shift to P and opened the door. The two women stood up. I smiled nervously. I was shy. It felt funny to meet somebody from the Internet in person.

"Are you Rhawnie and Corinna?" I said.

"Yep," they said together.

"I'm Kyle. This is my mom and my girlfriend, Dom."

"Hi," they said.

"Hi," we said.

We smiled and acted nice. It was like the first day of school. We small-talked for a few minutes then Corinna said, "So where's the red paperclip?"

"Ah yes, are you guys excited to make the trade?" I said.

"Oh for sure, we're always up for trading a fish pen for a red paperclip," Corinna said, and laughed.

"So, where did you say you found the fish pen?" I said.

"We were up on the Sunshine Coast at a music festival called Bonfire, and Rhawnie found it on the ground," Corinna said.

"Yep," Rhawnie said.

I pulled the red paperclip from my pocket. I looked at it for a moment. Then I held it out and said, "Here it is!"

Corinna looked at it for a moment, smiled and said, "It's so much nicer than I thought it'd be."

We laughed, and they handed over the fish pen.

I'd just made a trade.

Mom snapped a picture of the "three traders".

"So what are you going to do with the red paperclip?" I asked.

Rhawnie said, "Probably tape it to our fridge."

"What are *you* going to do with the fish pen?" Corinna said.

I thought about it for a moment and smiled. "I'm gonna trade it."

"With who?" Rhawnie said.

"I have no idea. I guess whoever calls next!" I said.

"That's such a rad way to look at things," Corinna said.

"But then again, I won't have the fish pen anymore," I said.

"It is just a fish pen," she said.

"Good point," I said.

There was a slight awkward silence. I said, "I remember in high school some people played a game like this and ended up with a car in a single day."

"That'd be so sweet if you could trade up to a car today," Rhawnie said.

I laughed and said, "Yeah, that'd be pretty cool. But I'm going to Seattle later today and taking a flight outta Sea-Tac tomorrow. I don't think you can check cars on airplanes. Yet."

We all laughed, because it was silly. *Yet* is like that. I looked over at Dom. "We should probably head out, I said, "Dom's got a flight to catch."

Rhawnie said, "Yeah, I've gotta go to work."

"Do you need a ride?" Mom said.

"I'm headed the other way than the airport. I'll take the SkyTrain," Rhawnie said.

"Can we give you a lift to the station? It's on our way," I said.

"Sure," she said.

With Rhawnie in the van, we pulled out of the parking lot. Corinna waved goodbye.

We drove past Bon's Off Broadway, a legendary all-day breakfast joint on the east side of Vancouver. With my hunger in mind, I turned around to Rhawnie in the back seat, "Hey, you guys ever go to Bon's?"

"What's Bon's?" she said.

"It's this place that has these crazy huge breakfasts for like two ninety-nine. Bacon, eggs, sausage, potatoes. It's *the best*," I said.

"You don't know about Bon's?" said Dom.

Mom nodded in agreement with Dom's and my fascination of Bon's spectacular breakfasts and looked eagerly at Rhawnie. Rhawnie looked a bit nervous and said, "Um, Corinna and I are pretty much vegans, so we probably wouldn't really be into that."

"Oh, I see," I said and bit my lip. I guess *that* explained their lack of sev burgers when we pulled into the parking lot. We arrived at the SkyTrain station. Rhawnie hopped out of the van. Well, actually, she stepped out of the van; hopped just sounds way more fun. We waved goodbye and pulled away.

"They were nice!" Mom said.

"They sure were," I said.

"That was fun!" she added.

"It sure was," I said.

The fish pen sat on the dashboard. Dom picked it up and held it in her hands. The wood was serrated, and when you moved it from side to side the fish looked like it was swimming.

Dom marvelled at the wooden fish and asked, "So, what do you think you'll trade it for?"

I thought about it for a second. I had no idea. I smiled and thought of the possibilities, "I don't know. That's the best part. The phone could ring right now and it could change everything. I put an ad for it in the barter section of the Seattle Craigslist the other day, so maybe we'll make a trade with somebody down there."

I squinted at a traffic light in the distance. It turned yellow. My foot came off the gas. As we started to slow down, my phone rang, or I should say, whinnied. My ringtone was set to "horse". Not sure which breed though. Dom said stallion; I said palomino. It's quite the discussion. I flipped the phone open.

"Hello?"

"Hi, is this Kyle?" A woman's voice came through the earpiece.

"Yep, that's me," I said.

The light went red.

The woman told me her name was Annie. "I saw your ad on Craigslist and want to trade with you," she said.

"You do?" I eased my foot onto the brake pedal.

"Yeah, I really like the sound of that red paperclip!" she said.

"Um, well, I just traded the red paperclip away though."

"Oh."

The van came to a stop.

"With who?" she asked.

"Two girls up here in Vancouver."

"Oh." There was a pause. Annie's voice came back. "Are you still making trades for red paperclips?"

"Well, sort of. I only had one red paperclip and I traded it for a pen shaped like a fish. So now I'd like to trade the fish pen for something."

"That sounds pretty cool," she said.

"Yes. It's a *great* fish pen," I said.

"Your ad in Craigslist said you'll be in Seattle today. Is that right?" she said.

"Yeah, I've got a flight early tomorrow morning out of Sea-Tac back to Montreal. We'll be in Seattle this afternoon. Wanna make a trade for the fish pen?"

"Yeah, I've got a houseful of stuff to trade."

"Sounds good. Do you mind if I drop by with my family?"

"No problem, come on by! Bring everybody!" She gave me her cross streets and said to call when we were in her neighborhood.

"Great, we'll see you this afternoon."

"See you then."

Dom looked over at me, "Who was that?"

"That was Annie. She lives in Seattle. We're going to trade this afternoon."

"Fun!" said Mom.

"Sounds good!" said Dom.

I looked up at the traffic light. It turned from red to green. I smiled and stepped on the gas.

Just trade it.

You can talk and plan and scheme and design and worry and come up with excuses until the cows come home. But at some point you'll realize that unless you're a farmer you don't own any cows and it's probably a bit of a long shot that cows will miraculously appear at your doorstep to signify that something is supposed to happen. If you want it to happen, you need to act on your idea.

Now was two words ago.

Yep, this is just a blatantly inane comment to make you think way-too-deep thoughts. But it's not. Unless you think it is. Then it is. If you want to analyze it, and give it meaning, that's fine by me. But analysis and deep thoughts won't change the simple new fact: Now was actually more like five words ago.

If you want it, go get it.

Nobody's going to hand it to you on a silver platter. It's not that people *don't* like to put things on silver platters and give them to people. *That* actually seems like a lot of fun. It's just that most people don't *have* silver platters.

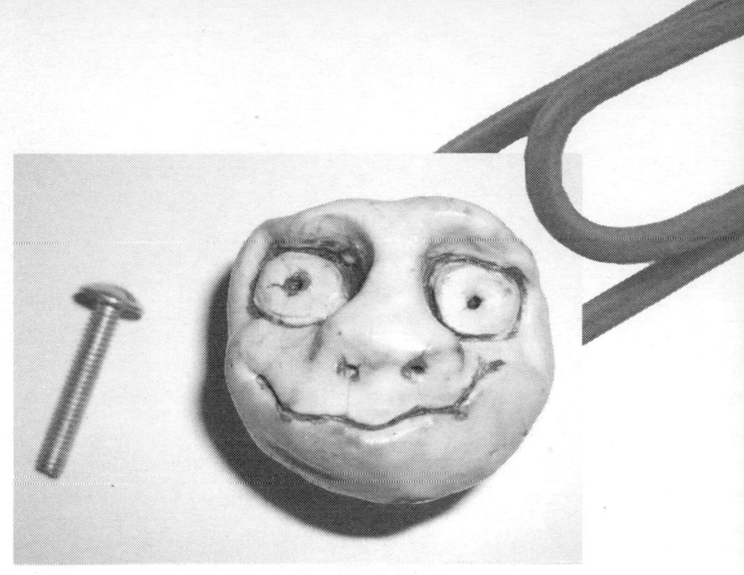

one doorknob

It was a full van. I drove. Mom rode shotgun. Dad, my brother, Scott, and his girlfriend, Rachel, and my grandpa were in the back. We were on I-5 headed south, just north of Seattle. We turned off I-5 at the Ballard exit. We were running late. If we stayed too long with Annie to make the trade, we'd miss the Mariners game. We had to make the game, because it justified the trip to Seattle. Without the game, we'd all just have piled into the van to give me a lift to Sea-Tac airport. If we went to the game, then it made sense to stay the night and make the trip to Seattle. I considered calling Annie to cancel the trade, but never did. It could all be done with some delicate timing. The rest of the van was in low-blood-sugar, let's-get-this-over-with mode, while I was in this'll-be-fun-guys!-justify-what-they-see-as-a-time-wasting-detour-while-already-late mode. Dad, on an empty stomach, was well into question-his-son's-motives-and-question-the-purpose-of-the-trip-to-Seattle mode. He said, "Turn down the radio for a second."

I did.

"So let me get this straight, Dom flew out of Vancouver and you have a flight out of Seattle tomorrow, right?"

"Right," I said.

"Tell me again, why didn't you go on the same flight as her?" he said.

He'd bought Dom and me flights from Montreal, and I was very thankful for that. I just made sure I'd found the lowest ticket price when I booked the flights.

"I booked my flight a few days after Dom, and by then a flight from Vancouver to Montreal cost twice as much as one from Seattle. You guys said you wanted to see a Mariners game, so it worked out perfectly, win-win, right?" I looked in the rearview mirror.

"Right," he said, unconvinced.

A moment later he said, "I didn't know there were direct flights from Seattle to Montreal."

"Oh, I don't think there are. I've got a stopover," I said.

"Where, O'Hare or something?" he asked.

"No, Vancouver," I said.

I smiled, because I thought it was funny how a flight from Seattle to Montreal with a stopover in Vancouver was half the price of a flight from Vancouver to Montreal.

Dad shook his head. "Now that's ridiculous."

Usually he'd find this sort of thing funny, one of those "life's like that" things. But today was one of those "life shouldn't be like that" kind of days for him. I think he'd just sat in the back of the van too long. For a guy who'd just encouraged me to trade my red paperclip, he sure wasn't being very enthusiastic about things. I turned the radio up.

Mom tried to change the subject. She held out a hairbrush and said, "You can't show up at somebody's house like that. You should brush your hair."

Now, I'm more than proud to say that my mom cuts my hair, because she does, but I can't stand it when she wants me to brush it. My hair doesn't brush well. She tried to force the brush into my hair. I tried to snag the brush and toss it somewhere preferable. Like into oncoming traffic.

As we got closer to Annie's place, Dad chimed in: "Let's make it quick. We don't want to miss the game."

I realized then that I didn't have Annie's exact address, just the cross streets. I got as near as my pen-on-the-back-of-my-hand notes could get us, then pulled the van to the side of the street and called Annie.

She answered, "Hello? Is that Kyle?" Just then a woman ran out of the house next to us, a cordless phone held to her head, and said, "Where are you?"

A split second later I heard "Where are you?" in my ear, I flipped the phone shut and leaned out the window. "Hey Annie."

Annie hung up her phone and walked toward the van. The sliding doors opened and everyone began to pile out. Annie's eyes bulged. "Yikes. I didn't realize so many of you were going to come here."

I was now on the sidewalk, next to Grandpa. I said to Annie, "Yeah, I guess you could say we like to roll deep, right Grandpa?"

He looked over at me, smiled and said, "That's right."

Annie was happy to see us there. I think she was a wee bit shocked by the velocity with which a vanload of strangers had materialized in front of her house. I had the feeling that vanloads of strangers didn't materialize in front of her house everyday. But then again, we'd only just met, so maybe they did. We walked inside the wooden house with the large front porch.

Annie held her arms out to welcome us in. "Welcome to my house. I, um, didn't have a chance to clean or anything."

I looked around. It was messy, but in a clean sort of way. Or maybe it was clean in a messy sort of way. It looked normal to me.

I said, "No worries, we can't stay long anyhow. We're on our way to the Mariners game."

Annie said, "Well, let's get down to business then. I have so many things that we could trade."

"Oh yeah? What kind of stuff?" I said.

"Well, follow me. I've got a few things set out."

I followed her to the kitchen, where, sure enough, some things were laid out on the countertop. There was a vase, a door-knob, a spoon and a banana.

I pulled out the fish pen and asked, "So what do you think about the fish pen?"

"It's cool. I just want to trade. It really doesn't matter what you have," she said.

"Check this out," I said and showed her how the fish swam when moved back and forth.

"It looks like it's swimming!" she said.

"Yep, just like a fish," I said.

Annie gestured at the objects laid out on the counter and said, "So what do you think? You've got a lot of choices here."

I put my hand on my chin with my thumb and forefingers on opposite sides of my mouth in a classic, about-to-make-a-decision pose. This was serious. If I made the wrong choice now and picked something nobody would want, the game of Bigger and Better would be over and I'd have to start all over again. Yes, this was a very serious decision. I thought about how I looked for a second, and lapsed from my faux decision-maker pose. Who was I kidding? I'd only made one trade. It literally didn't matter what I chose. It was just fun to be here. I looked down on the counter and grabbed the doorknob. It had a scrunched-up smiley face and just seemed like a nice doorknob.

I said, "I'll go for the doorknob."

"Good, it's a deal then!" said Annie.

We swapped the fish pen for the doorknob, shook hands, and Mom took our picture.

"You know what I *really* wanted to trade you for that fish pen?" Annie said.

"What's that?"

She pointed to the massive piece of painted steel in her kitchen and said, "My fridge."

I looked at it for a moment and imagined how it could work. I chuckled and said, "I'd totally be up for it, except I don't think *they* will let me take a fridge as carry-on baggage tomorrow. Checked? Maybe. But I really don't like to check luggage."

Annie smiled, a courtesy smile even. I think I saw a slight bit of sadness in her expression. I think she really wanted to trade her fridge for the fish pen. That, or find somebody gullible enough to haul it away for free in their van.

She gave us a tour of her garden and showed us some of her ceramic work. Her house was across the street from a park in Ballard, a suburb of Seattle. A really nice area. It was one of those early-twentieth-century neighbourhoods with streets on a grid, houses with porch stoops, and roundabouts with gardens in the middle. Annie's garden was kept in the classic do-more-important-things-than-obsess-about-pulling-weeds style. The grass fringe between the sidewalk and the street was a berm created from composting flowers, plants and leftover ceramic art. Annie had oodles of stuff lying about and gave us things to take away, as gifts. She pulled a vase from the ground and handed it to Mom. Mom accepted, saying thanks. Then she lifted an old dirty comb from the sidewalk, shined it on her leg and offered it to me. I examined the freshly brushed-off comb for a moment and nodded my head. Yep, Annie had just pulled a comb off the sidewalk, brushed it on her pant leg, and offered it to me. Was it a not-so-subtle hint for me to brush my hair? I looked over at Mom. Maybe she was right after all. She smiled and made one of those eyebrow-lifted, finger-extended, I-told-you-so Mom faces. I put the comb in my pocket. Maybe I'd brush my hair later and make her happy. That, or throw the comb into oncoming traffic.

I looked at Annie and said, "Well, I hate to trade and run, but we're going to be late for the Mariners game if we don't head out now. And I know how excited Rachel is about seeing her first big league game."

Rachel rolled her eyes.

"That's cool. It was great that you guys stopped by!" Annie said.

"Thanks for having us over!" Mom said.

Annie said, "So what do you think you'll trade the doorknob for?"

I thought about it for a moment and realized I had no idea. "I have no idea, but I have a feeling it'll open a few doors."

I think Mom let out a slight groan, and Scott did a Johnny-Carson-late-night-talkshow-punch-line-accentuating "rim shot" sound. It was tacky, but I think it's always better to add a cheesy metaphorical visualization to things whenever possible.

I added, "I'm going to trade it for something bigger or better."

"Cool! Do you know who you're going to trade with yet?" Annie asked.

"Not yet."

Annie pointed to a black Mercedes parked against the curb and said, "If you ever trade up to something good enough, I'll trade you my car!"

We looked at her car. It had seen better days, but it *was* a Mercedes. I looked at the doorknob in my hand, "If I can turn this doorknob into something worthy of your car, then I'll definitely give you a call!"

"Please do, and keep in touch!" she said.

"Will do."

We said goodbye to Annie and walked over to the van. I jumped up behind the steering wheel, but Dad came around to the driver's door and held out his hand for the keys. "Hop in the back, bucko."

I did.

Once we were on the road again, I felt a smug confidence. I'd just made my second trade of the day. A doorknob was bigger *and* better than a red paperclip. But most of all, we'd had fun. Everyone was excited.

Dad said, "That was pretty cool. Annie was great."

Mom said, "Nice comb she gave you, hey honey?"

We all laughed, and I said, "Yeah, you won that round Mom, but I'm still not brushing my hair."

"I don't think you should brush it with that one anyhow. It was on the sidewalk," she said.

I sensed a good time to turn the tables on her hair-brushing logic. "Well, maybe I *will* brush my hair with it then," I said.

"No, please don't."

"Okay I won't. I'll just throw it into oncoming traffic then."

She looked back at me with her teacher/Mom index finger extended to maximum-effective length, and said, "You better not."

I smiled and said, "So, changing the subject, how about her car? How cool would it be to go back one day and trade something for her car?!"

Mom, satisfied the comb was neither near my head nor in oncoming traffic, smiled, and said, "Can you imagine?"

I thought about it for a second. I could definitely imagine that. I said, "Yes, I can imagine that."

"That would be pretty cool," said Dad.

"So how about today? Two trades in one day. Not bad, huh?" I said.

Scott chimed in, "Yep, but all you have is a doorknob."

"Yeah, but it's got a pretty sweet smiley face on it," I said.

"I guess you could call it sweet."

"Anyhow, It's way better than a red paperclip," I said.

"Yep, you have a point there," Scott said in his sarcastic, whiney voice. He outstretched his arm and raised his hand in the air, palm up. "Besides, one man's trash is another man's treasure." He made a creepy chuckle.

I joined him with my own cheeseball voice. I raised my right index finger in the air and said in the most politically correct tone I could drum up, "You mean, one *woman's* trash is a another *man's*, treasure," and looked over at Rachel with fire in my eyes.

Rachel laughed, nervously.

Scott shook his head and said, "Aw man."

We didn't say much after that. We were hungry. And my last

remark sealed the deal that our conversation had pretty much bottomed out.

We sat in the lower-level stands at Safeco Field, near the foul pole in right field. As Ichiro Suzuki, a star Japanese player for the Mariners, stepped up to the plate, a group of young Japanese girls beside us began to cheer wildly. "I-CHI-RO! I-CHI-RO!" they screamed. The chant was almost hypnotic. The girls pulled disposable cameras and took pictures of him, more than three hundred feet away. I imagined just how un-Ichiro, he'd look after they developed the pictures. *Very* un-Ichiro, I decided.

Then I thought about how good today was. Very good. Up until now, "tomorrow" had been just a continually never-realized day. I'd put off "tomorrow" for a long time. But today was the day. Tomorrow had just happened. I'd traded my red paperclip and had tons of fun. I'd met three really cool people and gone to new places. I'd even wound up with a doorknob. I thought about how it would've been cool to hang out with Annie longer, but figured even a short encounter was better than nothing.

"I-CHI-RO! I-CHI-RO!" the girls screamed.

Scott poked me on the shoulder and I was roused from my thoughts. He smiled and pointed to the right. Grandpa was at the end of the row of seats, making his way through the throng of Ichiro fans. He smiled at the screaming girls. He had something in his hands. He made it over to us, held out two cardboard boxes, and said, "Would you boys like some Cracker Jack?"

"Yes please!" we said in unison.

Yes, today was a good day. But I couldn't wait to see what tomorrow would bring. Tomorrow was going to rock.

I've heard it before, but I want to hear it again. Differently.
Most new stories are variations of stories already told. But if you get caught up in how your story is similar to others it will just discourage you. The trick is to think about how your story is different. And tell it.

Now is now. And now. And now.
And it'll be *now* later on too. *Now* is sort of a continual gray area of time, sandwiched between *then* and *yet. Now* is quite plentiful really, so it's not like you need to worry and stress to take advantage of *now*. But if you don't take advantage of *now*, it becomes *then*. The trick is to see *yet* as it approaches, take advantage of *yet* as it becomes *now*, and turn *now* into a *then* when you arrive at a new *now*. But by far, the best *now* of all is *now*.

The easiest person to convince is you.
Unless, of course, you have a really gullible younger brother or something like that. Your thoughts and ideas are really great. Especially to you. And that's nice. You can talk all you want, but the only way you'll convince somebody else, is if you do something to make your ideas real.

one camping stove

And tomorrow *did* rock! Hard.

When I got back to Montreal I yanked my old decrepit cabinet knob from the cabinet below the sink. I screwed the new knob on and watched the cabinet door open. It was amazing. I caught sight of the solvents. I closed the door and opened it again. Yep, there they were. The solvents. Just loving it. I thought about how happy the solvents must be to have a smiley-faced knob on their cabinet door. I know if I were a solvent, I'd definitely be happy about that. I smiled. Then I remembered I planned to trade the doorknob away as soon as possible and thought how that might upset the solvents. I figured it was probably best to keep them out of the loop as far as my doorknob-trading plans were concerned. After all, they were deadly. But they'd get over it. They always do.

I went to the computer and checked my email. By now, my inbox was filled with offers for the red paperclip from my relentless Craigslist-spamming postings. More than one hundred people had made an offer for it. I emailed everyone and broke the bad news. The red paperclip was gone ... but if they still wanted to trade, I now had a doorknob that looked like a tripped-out version of ET crossed with a doorknob bred for its skills and magic, of course. Most people had thought the original Craigslist ad for one red paperclip was a joke. Not very many people thought I really wanted to trade the paperclip. I got dozens of sarcastic replies to the email: "Sorry, I'm not interested in the doorknob. I *really* had my eye on that red paperclip."

But some real offers came in too:

*****Well, I have ALWAYS wanted a tripped-out version of E.T. crossed with a doorknob ... bred for its skills and magic. Wanna trade it for a pretty Kitty in Milwaukee, WI? I will also throw in a Bud Select or two.... This is a real cat. A sweet, stray cat that I found and have kept because she was pregnant. Now the babies are born, weened, and adopted out and I have to find a home for the mom. (My roomie is allergic.) Not only is this a great excuse for you to come to Milwaukee, but also a good way to find a good home for the cat. (I haven't had much luck.) Only someone who really wants a cat would trade you for something bigger and better.
:) Brandis

*****Kyle,
I was spamming my site around the empty international craigslist sites (no I dont feel bad about it, no one local uses craigslist there) However, I bumped into your site from your tokyo listing. I wouldnt have wanted the pen anyhow – it was bombass though. The knob has my fancy and while I should hold out and wait for something better, but I can not hold myself back. Things i would happily trade for it ...
– A plaster model of a druken salor with his mouth open and hand out (put the bottle in his mouth and hand for storage).
I am a lazy self employed bum in Austin Texas.
Nathan

So I had my choice of a "druken salor" statue from a lazy, self-employed bum in Austin, Texas, or a stray cat fresh off maternity leave in Milwaukee. Every ounce of my funny bone wanted to make a spur-of-the-moment trip to Wisconsin to rescue a random cat or help clear the clutter for a Craigslist-spamming lazy self-employed bum in Texas, but it just wasn't going to happen. I was broke. The trade had to be close to home in Montreal or to fit with my travel plans. The following week I was going to New York with a friend named Allan. Anything between Montreal and New York would be perfect. I put ads for the doorknob on the barter section of every "relevant" Craigslist on the six-hour drive corridor between Montreal and New York.

I suddenly realized how my life was sort of like a real-life Choose Your Own Adventure book. Anything could happen. There were so many options. Each trade led to a different adventure. But I couldn't use an index finger to mark my page and read ahead down multiple plot lines to find the best option. I couldn't cheat Bigger and Better. My trades had to be real. Once I made a trade, I had to stick with it. I had to be careful, one wrong move and I'd be sucked into the equivalent of a black hole scary enough to a make a third-grade student cringe during forced-reading period.

The trades seemed to choose themselves. Some people had larger-than-life personalities in their emails, and I was keen to find out more about them and make a trade. Others were situated in geographically convenient locations. Shawn, from western Massachusetts, had both the personality and location:

*******Kyle,**

I REALLY like the knob. It would be the perfect knob for the top of my espresso maker. I HAVE to have it ... I'll trade you something really great for it ... I'll give you a two burner Coleman

camping stove. That's wayyyy bigger, and much better ... it's a pretty great leap from the paperclip, fish pen or knob ... but I really like the knob and am fascinated by your sociological experiment. .. After looking at your blog, you seem like a very interesting person ... I hope you do well in life with such a care-free spirit. (I'm totally not a hippy, or hitting on you ... but I couldn't figure out a way to comment on that without sounding like either.) By the way ... I have always lived my life on the barter system ... the car I'm driving now, 1993 Chevy Blazer ... yeah, I got it for an old laptop that I bought at the beginning of my school career three years ago.

A camping stove? Now we're talking. And what was this *by the way I traded my laptop for a truck*? Shawn was the kind of guy I had to meet. A real trader. I was enticed. I replied:

Shawn,
thanks for the non-hippy, not-hitting-on-me disclaimer. Way easier to get that out of the way than let it linger. Nice tactic. Whereabouts in Western Mass do you live?

Shawn:
In Amherst ... If you score me the doorknob, I'll toss in a cold beer as well.

The enticement deepened.

Kyle:
Perfect. I'll be there next week. Is Monday the 25th around noon/afternoon good for you?

Shawn:

Sounds great, I'll be around. If you need to call for any bizarre reason ...

And he gave me his number. I tried to think of the sort of bizarre reason that would warrant a call to Shawn, but drew a blank. I jotted down the number anyhow. Maybe I'd think of a bizarre reason later. I'm usually quite good at coming up with bizarre reasons for things.

Dom came into the room, very timely, and asked, "So, Mister Doorknob, what's your next trade?"

"A Coleman stove."

"Huh? *C'est quoi ça?*" she said.

"Um, it's like a little gas stove. You know, for camping?"

"Ah, *oui, un four à camping.*"

"Yeah, that's it."

"Where are you going to get this *four à camping?*"

"Amherst," I said.

Dom shot me a confused look and said, "What is that, *H*amherst?" In addition to possessing a Québecoise accent that adds the letter *H* to all words that begin with a vowel and removes the letter *H* from all words that begin with the letter *H*, Dom has a way of being totally blown away by things she doesn't know. The name *Amherst* was a bit of a shock to her system. I'm sure she'd never heard it before.

"Let me show you." And I pulled up a map and showed her where Amherst was.

"Ah, it's in *Massachusetts.*"

"Yep."

"When are you going there?"

"Soon, very soon."

*

Soon after that, Allan and I rolled up to Shawn's place in Amherst in our red Corolla. It was late in the afternoon. And hot. And humid. Shawn wasn't home yet. I looked over at the carport and eyed the camping stove. Allan saw it too. He said, "Hey there's your stove! Wanna go grab it and we can take some pictures?"

"No, I want to wait for Shawn. If I don't scope it out now, it'll be a lot easier for me to pretend later that I'm seeing it for the first time," I said.

A red Chevy Blazer driven by someone I assumed to be Shawn pulled into the driveway and came to a stop. From the passenger door, a shirtless kung fu warrior tore out of the truck. "Hiiiiya!" screamed the little boy. He swung fists in our direction. Fire was in his eyes. He ran over and said, "Who are you guys?!" He shot a roundhouse kick at Allan's knee and punched the air in front of me with careful precision.

I said, "My name's Kyle and this is Allan. We're here to make a trade."

"Really!? What kind of trade?" the boy asked.

"Well, I thought we came here to trade this doorknob for a camping stove. How does that sound?"

"A doorknob?" he said.

"Yup, a doorknob," I said.

His forehead scrunched up and he looked at the Blazer. "Dad, why do we need a doorknob?"

Dad stepped out of the truck. "Well, buddy, it's a knob that I'm going to put on my espresso maker."

"Huh, cool," said the kung fu warrior. His eye caught something interesting in the distance. He shot off to check it out. Dad extended his right hand. "Hey, you're Kyle. I'm Shawn. I recognize you from the website. And this is..."

"Allan," said Allan.

"Cool. Good to meet you guys. Glad you could make it. That's Seamus, my son. He just had swimming practice. He's a little more riled up than usual."

Shawn reached into the six-pack tucked under his arm, and pulled out a bottle. It looked cold. He raised his eyebrows.

"Yes please," we said.

"So are you guys hungry?" he asked.

"Oh yes," we said.

"The camping stove is right over there," said Shawn as he opened his beer. "I'm sure you guys already took pictures of it and everything."

I looked at the camping stove and said, "Yes. Right. There it is. Just over there. No, we didn't get any pictures yet."

Shawn looked indifferent. "I think we should make the trade before we eat, get it out of the way, you know."

I reached into my pocket, pulled out the doorknob, and said, "Here's your doorknob."

Shawn looked at the doorknob, then up at me. A streak of concern came across his face. "Hang on a second. I can't trade with you yet."

"Why not?" I said.

He smirked slightly. "You're not wearing your trading shirt."

"My trading shirt?" I said.

"Yeah, your striped shirt. The one you wear in the pictures on your website. You can't make a trade without your official trading shirt," Shawn said.

"Oh, you mean Ricky's shirt? It's not really my official trading shirt or anything. I just happened to wear it for the first two trades."

Shawn was visibly let down. He dropped his head slightly. "Oh. I thought you wore it to all the trades."

I didn't want to upset Shawn, so I said, "Well, it's not my official trading shirt, but maybe it should be, shouldn't it?"

He raised his head slightly, hope in his eyes, and said, "It is your lucky shirt, isn't it?"

I thought about it for a second and said, "I guess it is my lucky shirt. Well, actually, no. It's Ricky's lucky shirt, I was just wearing it for him."

Shawn said hopefully, "Did you bring it?"

"Yeah, it's in my car," I said, and I did that cool, thumb-over-my-shoulder, beer-in-the-other-hand gesture to unnecessarily indicate to Shawn that my car was behind me.

"What are you waiting for? Do you wanna trade or not?" he said.

I spun around, ran to the car and threw Ricky's shirt on my back. I was glad that I had packed it in the car. Not just glad, super glad. Shawn was right. I did need a lucky trading shirt. And the way things were going, Ricky's shirt was proving to be lucky.

Allan took pictures of us as we "made the trade". The exact sort of cheesy pictures you'd expect.

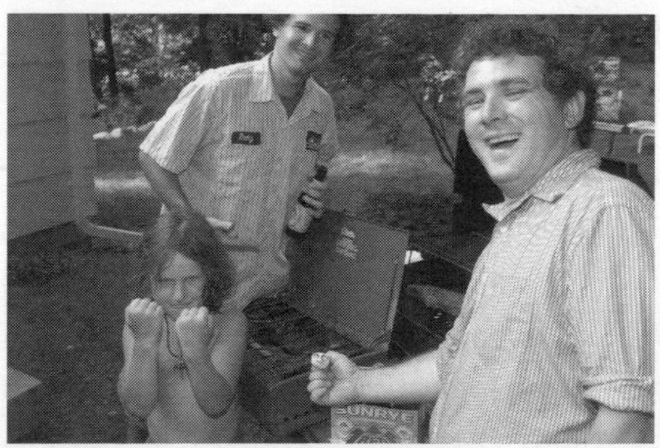

Shawn threw in a can of stove fuel with the deal, so now it was a camping stove *with fuel.*

Black Belt Jones – I mean Seamus – came back for the second round. He did Bruce Lee ninja moves for the camera. He loved the camera. He loved attention.

We stood over the barbecue as the steaks cooked. I asked Shawn, "So is it true you traded a laptop for your truck?"

Shawn pointed at his truck and said, "That one right there. Pretty cool huh?" He pointed at the house. "See this house? House-sitting gig. Craigslist."

Shawn talked the talk, walked the walk, and housed the house. He ruled. Shawn had the special spark. He was a catalyst. He made me want to go out and catalyze things. Shawn was a legendary trader. Here I was, all excited to swap a doorknob for an unwanted camping stove, and the guy in front of me points at a truck he scored for an old laptop. I was definitely speaking to an experienced trader. Shawn was originally from the Bay area. A dynamic guy. Hyperactive and laid back. Easy going but brimming with energy. An ideas man, for sure. Being there with Shawn confirmed that Bigger and Better had legs. But Bigger and Better wasn't just an idea anymore, it was real. I realized my trades might not be a series of one-off Craigslist flukes, after all. Shawn actually wanted to help me trade up to a house.

I took a big sip of beer. Shawn said, "Good thing you guys came when you did, 'cause my course at UMASS just ended and I'm moving to DC in two weeks."

"What were you taking at UMASS?" I asked.

"Journalism," he said, and continued, "Yeah, I'm moving there in my truck and there's not much room for stuff. I have another camping stove but there's only enough room for one of 'em in the truck, so I actually tried to sell the camping stove at a garage sale the other week. Nobody went for it, so I left it on the side of the road with a 'free' sign on it. There were no takers there either. But then I saw your ad in the barter section of Craigslist and fired you an email. I figured I could help you trade up!"

"I'm glad you didn't sell it!" I said.

Shawn, Seamus, Allan and I tore into hearty steak sandwiches the size of hush puppies. Best steak sandwich I ever ate. I made a mental note to get more doorknobs. We tried to muscle the broken old knob off Shawn's espresso maker with greasy hands and a kitchen knife, but it wouldn't budge. Shawn looked up and said, "I'll find some pliers and yank it off later. I can send you a picture if you'd like."

I finished my bite and said, "Sure, that'd be great. Not as great as this steak sandwich though."

Shawn smiled and looked at the doorknob. "It'd be cool if we could put the new knob on right now, but you can't win 'em all."

Shawn wanted to talk. He wanted to share something with us.

Seamus had just run off and left his half-finished steak sandwich on the table, Shawn called after him, "Seamus, are you going to finish your dinner?"

"Daaad. I'm not hungry," Seamus said.

"Buddy, I think you should come and finish it. Please?"

Seamus rolled his eyes and ran back and hammered away at the sandwich with renewed vigour. Shawn looked at him with a proud but pensive face. I couldn't help but think something else was on Shawn's mind. Shawn had worried over more than getting rid of the camping stove. Seamus downed his last bite and ran off to practise free-style martial arts on a full stomach. Shawn watched him round the corner, looked over at us, and said, "Yeah, Seamus is going to live with his mom in San Francisco. I haven't told him yet."

I took a swig of beer.

"He leaves next week," he added.

I swallowed. I couldn't imagine what separation was like. My parents were together. They'd always been together. It must be really tough, especially being away from your kids. I felt guilty to be spending time with Shawn. He had only one week left with his son. But it was clear he wanted to talk and hang out with us. He lit a cigarette. It was a strange situation. He clearly enjoyed the company. The fact we were total strangers must have brought a breath of fresh air into a rough time in his life. He wanted to take a breather ... albeit with a cigarette in his mouth.

Shawn had nervous energy, but Seamus had energy energy. Energy that intensified with a bellyful of meat. Shawn eyed Seamus coming toward the table with a garden hose in his hand and tucked his cigarette under the picnic table.

Seamus was ready to strike. "Hey, Dad, when can we play?"

"We'll play soon enough, dude. Why don't you go and water the plants on the front side of the house first?"

Seamus curled up his mouth to disapprove of the idea but Shawn raised his eyebrows and shrugged his shoulders as if to say, *I don't like it either pal, but that's the way it is.*

Seamus didn't want to push his luck, so he ran off to hydrate the plants. Shawn watched him round the corner of the house and took a big drag. He exhaled and said, "He doesn't know I smoke either."

Allan and I nodded our heads in gentle agreement with Shawn. We silently agreed that it was just "one of those things".

Shawn butted out his cigarette and looked at me. "How far do you think you'll go with this Bigger and Better thing?"

I thought about it for a moment, then said, "I don't know, maybe I'll trade up to something real cool. The idea is to trade stuff with people and just see where it goes. On my blog I said

I'd like to trade up to a house, but that was more for fun than anything."

Shawn shot a glance at the stove, then at his truck. He had an idea. "You know, I've got some buddies down in Baltimore who can probably hook you up with a computer if you make a few more up trades. If you get up to something better than the camping stove, they'll probably be up for it. I traded my laptop for that truck. I'm sure you can trade up to a used car if you get a computer."

"Yeah, I think it's possible. I just need to keep trading," I said.

"How often do you make trades?" Shawn asked.

"You're the third person I've traded with. I just started, really."

"That's why I wanted to give you the camping stove. Something with a bit of meat to it, no pun intended. You can trade pens and doorknobs forever. I just thought I'd hook you up with something actually bigger and better," he said.

I smiled and said, "Sure, the stove is bigger and better, but it won't help me open the lid on my stove-top espresso maker will it?"

Shawn smiled and said, "No, it won't."

"Thanks again for the stove. It's awesome." I smiled at Shawn and added, "I mean, I know it's left over from a garage sale and all, but I really appreciate it."

He smiled. "Yeah, no problem. It's not about the stuff. It's about hanging out together like this. Forget the stove. This is cool."

"For sure, I see the trade items as keys to adventure," I said.

"And beer," said Allan.

"Yeah, this didn't hurt either," I said, and clinked bottles with Shawn and Allan.

Shawn looked at the camping stove again. "You know, you

could keep going forever with this. There's no reason you ever need to stop. I bet if you keep at it long enough, you can get a house."

I swallowed. I'd thought about this before, right when I saw the red paperclip on my desk. I knew it was possible, but I planned to make trades for fun and see where things took me. I was – um, how do you say – maybe a little bit, uh, noncommittal. Why put total commitment into something that isn't meant to be, right? I wanted to test the depth of the water before I dove in. I didn't need to smash my head on the bottom of the pond right now. Besides, I knew it was possible to trade up to a house, but would it be fun? Anything is possible, but some things aren't worth the effort. Sure, I could make a series of trades for bigger or better objects until I got a house, but would the house at the end be worth enough to justify all the time and expense of making the trades? I envisioned myself shelling out thousands of dollars to shuttle increasingly expensive things around the country. First I'd trade the camping stove for an unwanted piano in Anchorage. Then I'd trade that for a 1995 Chevy Lumina with no hubcaps in Florida. If one thing was certain, at some point I'd wind up with a 1995 Chevy Lumina with no hubcaps. The hubcapless Lumina would go for a two-week timeshare in Hawaii, which I'd flip for a rotten trailer home in Newfoundland, which I'd finally swap for an unwanted locust-infected bayou bungalow in Louisiana. All the hassle would cost a fortune in shipping. I imagined how I'd work myself ragged to trade up to a house, have a great housewarming party, but then be forced to sell it right away to pay off the mountain of debt from shipping companies and exterminators. Maybe if I were lucky, and extremely shrewd with my trades, I could break even after the eventual sale of the house. I was sure I could trade up to a house, but I wasn't sure if I could deal with a bayou bungalow filled with locusts. I *can't stand* locusts.

Shawn brought me back to reality. "Just take your time, and see what happens. It's not like you have a deadline or anything. You can do this for the rest of your life if you want."

When Shawn said I could trade up to a house, it made things different. If *he* thought it was possible, if somebody other than me thought it was possible, if enough people thought it was possible – it was. It took more than one guy to get to the moon. If I blazed a trail and made it happen, more people would follow and make offers for my objects. If I met enough people like Shawn, maybe I could trade up to a house after all. And maybe, just maybe, I wouldn't have to sell it all at the end to pay off scads of debt. Or deal with locusts. Besides, up until now, I hadn't spent a cent on the project. But then again, up until now, all my trade items had fitted in my back pocket.

I shook my head to get back to reality. One look at the old camping stove wiped the image of a massive housewarming party out of my mind and brought me back pretty fast. Ah, reality. My old friend. In *reality*, I was a broke dreamer stupid enough to take an old camping stove off a guy about to move. In *reality*, I was an idiot. I was a free way for Shawn to get rid of his junk. Yep, plain and simple. I didn't have an amazing plan. I was a sucker. He probably just told me that warm and cosy story about the house just to make me forget about the camping stove.

Shawn must've seen the concern in my eyes. "You know, Kyle, you're onto something really cool here. Whether you trade up for something valuable or not, it's neat just to make trades and meet new people. You're going to have a great time doing this. I think you can do it." He raised his eyebrows and said, "After all, you do have a uniform." He lifted his bottle and said, "Here's to the journey."

"And the best steak sandwiches in Amherst," Allan said.

"You got that right," I said, and took a sip of beer. It was scorching. Not the beer, the weather. The beer was ice cold. A cold beer or a camping stove was much more valuable than a house right now. We were about to drive to New York, in a red Corolla. Houses don't fit in red Corollas.

A hose-free Seamus ran toward us. Shawn looked at him and said, "You ready for that game, bud?"

Allan and I waved goodbye to Shawn and Seamus. We promised to send Shawn copies of the pictures we had taken – especially the few dozen Allan snapped of Seamus doing awesome ninja moves. We hit the road in the red Corolla.

Shawn was right. The objects weren't the story; as clichéd as it sounded, it was about the journey. I thought about the expression "Every great journey begins with a single step." My journey started when I traded one red paperclip for one fish pen. One red paperclip was what I traded away to take my first step. It was then and there, as I steered the red Corolla past a large white house and towards the steamy sunset, in high spirits from the trade, that I decided to call Bigger and Better "one red paperclip". It was one red paperclip from here on out. One red paperclip was the symbol for where I came from and, more importantly, what I could do next. I could do anything next. I even had a uniform.

The more things change, the more they're different.
Yep, another inane line for you to overthink about. But think about it for a second. It's true.

Ask not what your mind can do for you, ask what you can do for your mind.
Sure, I cribbed it from J.F.K.'s speech. At least it was a good speech. Ask not how you can train your mind to work for you, ask how you can do things that will give you peace of mind. Does it feel right? If not, *how* can you make it feel right?

one red generator

When I returned to Montreal I had big plans. I posted little stories on my wesbsite about the trades with Rhawnie and Corinna, Annie, and Shawn. I uploaded pictures to help tell the story and let people know I wasn't just some sort of anonymous trade-seeking weirdo or spam dude. I was just a guy in Montreal with a camping stove. A guy who wanted to trade. My blog was still located on an obscure page of another website but I bought the domain www.oneredpaperclip.com and had it auto-forward from there so it was easier to find. I tweaked the blog to make it more user friendly. With simplicity in mind, I started to use the email address oneredpaperclip@gmail.com. I energetically transformed "Bigger and Better" into "one red paperclip". The name one red paperclip would set me apart. A name of my own. Yeah, that was the ticket. *Several dozen* people already visited oneredpaperclip.com every day, so I was practically on easy street. I figured the trade offers would roll in all by themselves, so I waited.

And waited.

And waited.

It was summer. The whole world was lazy. And so was I. The trade offers didn't exactly roll in like I thought they would, and even the ones that did only reinforced the idea that I should kick back and relax:

*****Yes, from one Kyle to another ... This morning, I was sitting back, relaxing on my wonderful red wing back chair (yes, it's not exactly a couch ... but i am ... if that counts) thinking about my life and any major holes in it ... then I remembered your email ... you know ... the one you sent me regarding my imminent need for a Coleman Stove ... At the time I thought, what an unfortunate situation, here is a Kyle with a perfectly good Coleman Stove (with fuel) and another Kyle seeking a perfectly good Coleman Stove ... but I was camping that weekend, and there was no time to pursue your stove at that time ... So it got me thinking ... you're a hard working guy ... looking to get a free house, and I thought to myself ... what makes a house a home ... well, furniture of course. So, I thought ... here I am, a camping sort of guy, minus the obligatory stove component to my kit ... why not trade. So, with that, I'm thrilled to offer you my wonderfully comfortable wing back chair for your Coleman Stove. I live in Toronto, so it's a bit of a trip, but we'll gladly feed you, and heck, you can even spend the night on the chair just to make sure you like it.
Kyle

*****How about one laz-y-boy for the paper clip and coleman stove. The laz-y-boy is a dusty rose colour. It is a rocking chair as well as a recliner. It is now available, so if you want it come and get it. Actually, if you want it, you better let me know asap, 'cause it might leave in the next two days, however, I'd be willing to hold it for you if you'd like it. I have many paper clips and I am sure the red one would be quite happy to hang out with my lime green, white, blue and plain paper clips. I often find them useful. And the coleman stove would replace the one I lost in the divorce. Then all I need is a tent and I could go camping again. That would be fun. Have a great day, I know I will.
Janet

*******I'll trade you a Book of the Mormon, five great volumes in Braille, for the Coleman. We'll provide the dogs and the burger 'n' chips at the cookout. Why the Braille books? The darn things are big enough to sit on as you go "blindly" in your quest for the biggest and bestest trade on Craigslist. I'll even show you how to read them so you won't get bored waiting for the next trade. Pictures available on request.**
Deb. Jericho, Vermont

I began to think that maybe I *wasn't* on easy street after all. It's not like I fell into a rut or didn't do anything; it's just that offers arrived only from afar, so I wasn't motivated to make trades because I didn't see a way I could do so. I routinely added a listing to the barter section for Craigslist in Montreal (and now adhered to Craigslist's anti-spam policy), but the English-language Craigslist didn't have much of a following in mainly French-speaking Montreal. And I hadn't lucked into a surprising stash of cash that would allow me to trade by commercial aircraft. I sat on the idea that I had to make the best of things when I was in different places.

At the end of August I got a call from my friend/part-time boss Evian.

"Do you want to work a trade show in Los Angeles next month?" he asked.

"Yes," I said.

One of the ways I'd occasionally strung together rent money was working very part-time gigs at trade shows around Canada and the United States to promote Table Shox, a shock-absorber device designed to stop restaurant tables from wobbling. It was the sort of gig that came up every month or two. Definitely not enough to cover the rent all the time, but it helped.

"Do you want to drive a van full of supplies down from Vancouver to get to Los Angeles?"

"Yes," I said.

It was perfect. There were many trade offers from people located in places along the 1,500-mile drive between Vancouver and Los Angeles. I emailed everyone between Vancouver and Los Angeles who'd made an offer and let them know I'd be in the area in a few weeks' time. I figured I could do my own little "trade shows" on the side.

In mid-September, I packed the camping stove and hopped on a plane for Vancouver. By the time I arrived on the West Coast, a few of the dozen trade offerers had emailed back:

*******HI,**
I live in san Clemente, California. Is the coleman stove with fuel still available? I may have some stuff to trade. If it isn't still available, what is the next item up for trade?
David

*******I am in SLC Utah, I have a '97 Honda civic engine and transmission I will trade you for the Coleman Stove.**
Matt

I knew the '97 Honda Civic package likely had a much higher street value than a little camping stove, but how would I re-trade, or transport, something like that? I ruled it out. I responded to David:

*******The coleman stove is still up for grabs. I'll be in LA/SanDiego sept 25th-ish, but might trade the stove by then ... what do you have in mind to trade?**
kyle

PS I'll keep you updated if I make a trade ...

David replied:

I have a honda 1000 watt generator. Portable, and only weighs about 50lbs so is easily carried one handed.
thanks,
david

Kyle:

Wow. That's a very interesting trade. Would you be willing to trade your honda generator for the coleman stove?

David:

Yeah, if you are willing to trade, i will tune it up for you, and fill up the gas tank.
thanks,
david

Now that was like it! A one-thousand-watt generator. No, better yet, a *tuned-up* one-thousand-watt generator, *with fuel.* Unless somebody made an unbeatable offer for the camping stove in the meantime, David was the guy.

It took a few days to complete the drive south from Vancouver to Los Angeles. Mom and Dad took a plane down to help out with the trade show, and we enjoyed the better part of three days' worth of trademark warm California indoor lighting from the interior of the Anaheim Convention Center. On a slow day, Mom and I slipped away from the trade show booth with the camping stove and drove the fifty or so miles south on I-5 to Camp Pendleton Marine Corps Base in San Clemente. I'd contacted David via email to confirm the trade. His directions included “It’s just before the Dolly Partons on I-5,” referring to the two blue domes on Interstate 5, that if looked at in the right way, were reminiscent of Dolly Parton. Or at least two parts of Dolly Parton. I don’t know what they are, but they look like two giant upturned blue breasts on the side of I-5. I remembered seeing them in the movie *The Naked Gun*, had recently driven past Camp Pendleton, and knew who Dolly Parton was, so I knew exactly what he was talking about. I saw them in the distance and took the exit off the highway.

It was the first time I’d ever gone to a military base with Mom. She was really nervous.

“I’m really nervous,” she said.

“Mom, it’ll be okay. Just hand me your passport,” I said.

We pulled out our passports, and I got my driver’s licence ready. We pulled up to the checkpoint. The guard approached the vehicle and eyed us cautiously.

“Hi, sir, how are you doing today?” he said.

“Fine, thank you,” I said.

“Can I see some identification please.”

“Yes, no problem.” I handed over our passports.

“What brings you to the base today?” he asked.

“I’m here to meet up with a marine sergeant,” I said.

“Who’s that?” he said.

“David,” I said.

He looked at the passports, sort of.

“Who?” he asked.

“He’s a sergeant, I think.”

“I don’t know him. How do you know him?” he said.

“We contacted each other. He’s selling a generator,” I said. Much easier to just say he was selling a generator than explain my whole story of trading up. In fact, I didn't even know how I *would* explain my whole story.

The guard looked down at the passports, this time more suspiciously. "You're both Canadian?" he said.

I was worried. We were foreigners. "Yes we are," I said.

He smiled and said, "Aw, that's cool. I'm from New York. I'm from real close to you guys."

"Yeah, we're from Vancouver, on the west coast," Mom said. I shot Mom a glance to cool it with the geographical accuracy of what part of Canada she lived in. I didn't want her to blow it.

"Yeah, sure, cool, hey you have a good day, alright?" he said. He looked at me and smiled. Then he almost winked. As if he knew something. Did he know I'd been living in Montreal, right above New York, for the last couple of years?

"No problem," I said.

"Pass on through," he said.

We drove through the residential part of the base. There were mobile homes on concrete pads everywhere, but it wasn't a trailer park. More like a cross between a trailer park and suburbia. It was either a trailer park with culs-de-sac and sidewalks, or suburbia without the trouble of permanent housing. I couldn't decide.

We pulled up to David's place. He stood in the driveway with one half of a hardtop for a Ford Bronco in his hands. His buddy was holding the other end. They lifted it into a trailer. There was stuff strewn all around. He was packing to move. I grabbed the camping stove, and we hopped out of the van and walked toward him.

"You must be Kyle," he said.

"Yep, that's me. This is my mom, Colleen."

"Pleased to meet you, ma'am," he said.

I saw her cringe. She doesn't like being called ma'am. Or sir, for that matter. We all shook hands and smiled.

"So you're moving or something?" I asked.

"Yeah, heading back to South Carolina," he said.

"You said lots of people have been dropping by?"

"Yeah, I'm trying to sell as much stuff as we can."

"I guess this trade will help you out then?" I said.

"I guess. You said you were trying to trade up to a house, and I thought I'd help you out," he said.

"Thanks!" I said.

"You had the model of Coleman stove I was looking for. It's not easy to find a good old one like that," he said.

I thought he might go one step further and say, *They don't make them like they used to* and cast an epic stare into the distance to remember the lost days of quality-manufactured camping stoves. But he didn't.

David added, "I've got a few generators, anyhow." He pointed to the side of the house.

There *were* a few generators – at least half a dozen. I cast him a look of intrigue.

"Military auction," he said.

He told me all about how the generator worked. He talked about "hertz", "cycles", AC and DC, and a bunch of other stuff I can't remember. I understood the words he said, but together they didn't make much sense. I nodded and scratched my chin hard enough until I was sure I'd convinced him that I had an appropriate "one of the boys" level of comprehension. He pulled the starter cord on the generator. It started on the first pull. And that was all I needed to know.

We all shook hands and Mom and I rolled out. Yep, just like my second favorite early 90s techno-rap group, Snap!, my Mom and I "got the power". She smiled and said, "Well, that wasn't so bad after all. I actually really enjoyed myself. Thanks for inviting me along."

"No problem," I said.

Over the next couple of days, Evian and I drove the van up I-5 to Portland, where my flight back to Montreal departed from. After a night at an airport hotel, we drained the fuel tank on the generator and arrived at the airport. I put the generator in a box and checked it as luggage. I waved goodbye to Evian, grabbed my boarding pass and walked through security to the gate. As I was about to scan my ticket and walk down the bridge to the plane, a booming voice on the airport PA system rang out: "Will Kyle MacDonald please report to the TSA security checkpoint. Once again, will Kyle MacDonald please report to the TSA security checkpoint."

Uh oh.

I put my boarding pass in my pocket and walked back

through security and onto the concourse. When I reached the TSA screening booth I found out that, even though they're not on the list of things not meant to be flown, a gasoline generator, drained of all fuel or not, is not meant to fly.

I looked at the TSA attendant and said, "I thought if I drained the fuel, it'd be okay."

The TSA attendant put her hands on her hips, leaned back, let out a slight laugh, and said, "It's not the fuel that's the problem. It's the fumes. The fumes are explosive. Gasoline is nothing. You can extinguish a lit match in a bowl of gasoline."

Wow. I really wanted to see her extinguish a lit match in a bowl of gasoline. I *so* didn't believe her. I was this close to asking for a demonstration when I remembered my flight. It was about to leave. I had to act fast. I pulled out my cell phone and called Evian at the hotel near the airport.

"Can you come to the airport and pick up the generator?" I said.

I'm sure he bit his lip and sucked it up. He knew why. "Be right there," he said.

Within minutes, he pulled up in the van and hopped out.

"Sorry man," I said.

"No problem."

I smiled and said, "Besides, you need to send stuff to Toronto for the trade show in a month, don't you?"

"Actually, I do. You gonna be there?" he said.

"Yep, I'll drive down from Montreal," I said.

He pointed at the generator and said, "I'll ship this bad boy with the trade show booth. Ground."

"Perfect. See you then." I looked down at the red generator, patted it affectionately, and said, "And I'll see *you* there too." As I started to walk away I turned and said to Evian, "Hey, do you know that you can extinguish a lit match in a bowl of gasoline?"

"What?" he said and shot me a look of disbelief.

I turned and yelled over my shoulder, "Yeah, apparently it's the fumes that are dangerous!" Then I ran and caught my flight. Barely.

A month later I made the five-hour drive from Montreal to Toronto. I met Evian at the hotel and, the next morning, we went to the trade show in our Table Shox shirts. The red generator was sitting in the booth. I examined it and looked up at Evian. "Looks like it made it here alright!"

"You going to try to extinguish a lit match in gasoline?" he said.

"Sure, just find me a match!" I said, "and some gasoline."

"I'd like to see it too, but not around the booth, please," he said.

"Okay."

I had to listen. He was the boss after all.

A couple of people in Toronto made offers for the generator, so after we'd hawked our solution to wobbly tables, we loaded it into my car and drove off to check them out.

We went to scope out a treadmill offered by a gent named Nick. We found Nick's house and knocked on the door. He was really excited to make the trade, and pointed to the treadmill in his garage. I looked at it and bit my lip. In the name of Bigger or Better, I was supposed to trade for bigger or better things, and the treadmill was definitely bigger than the generator. But it wasn't any better. It was rusty. And sketchy. A rough treadmill would be very hard to trade. I apologized to Nick and declined the trade. It's not like I really cared that much about the generator. I just didn't want to haul around a rusty treadmill until the end of time.

A few days of wobbly-table-solution hawking later, we packed up the trade show booth and I dropped Evian off at the airport for his flight back to Vancouver. On my drive back to Montreal I stopped in Scarborough, a suburb of Toronto, to meet up with Kevin, who'd offered a vending machine for the generator. In my mind a vending machine was the perfect trade item. A generator could generate power, but a vending machine could generate *money*. It was practically a money tree, but without all the messy leaves to deal with come fall.

Kevin pointed to the vending machine. It was massive. Like a refrigerator. But pink. And sketchy. It must've weighed at least five hundred pounds. I couldn't imagine how we'd ever lift it onto the roof of my car, let alone up the three flights of stairs to our apartment. But worst of all, it accepted only Canadian coins worth twenty-five cents or less. It wasn't even calibrated to accept loonies. Nope, not even *loonies.* I watched my dream of a leafless money tree fly away. I didn't want to limit my potential future trades to loonie-hating Canadian strongmen, so I said thanks but no thanks. Kevin understood and said, "Maybe next time."

"Definitely," I said.

We hung out for a while anyway, and Kevin gave me two T-shirts from his off-road-themed clothing company, Bush Pig.

"Wear them in good health," he said.

"I will," I said.

I drove back to Montreal. I felt somewhat bad that I hadn't made a trade in Toronto, because Nick and Kevin were both nice guys. But then again, I didn't want to open up a junkyard. The important thing was I got to hang out with them, and that was cool.

A week or so passed. The generator sat in our apartment. Offers rolled in but they were from far-off places. I tried to find places to advertise the generator in Montreal but the Craigslist in

Montreal didn't have the same number of readers as other large North American cities. I started to question my decision not to trade. Did I make a mistake? Maybe I should have traded for the treadmill or the vending machine. But I couldn't think along those lines. I could question myself forever, but it wouldn't solve anything. I had to forge ahead. There was no looking back. But the momentum was lost. The choose-my-own-adventure was now difficult. All this trading sure was fun when it was fresh, and easy, but now that I had to put constant effort into it to make it work, it had become less fun. The day I'd traded away my red paperclip was fun, but now the trades seemed like a chore. I felt ready to scrap the game, or at least put it on the back burner and find another way to pay the rent.

For the next two weeks I worked a few small contracts doing promotion work around Montreal for a marketing company. My paycheck from the trade show in Toronto was enough to cover the rent, and the contract for the marketing company put a bit of food on the table.

One evening, I sat across the table from Dom in a restaurant on Avenue Mont Royal. Food was on the table. My treat. A rare occasion.

"I might put one red paperclip on the back burner," I said.

"What do you mean?" she said.

I wasn't sure if she didn't get the "back burner" metaphor, or if she just wanted me to continue talking. Since I really didn't understand what it meant to put something on the back burner, or why that expression even existed in the first place, I decided to continue talking.

"The whole trading thing is really distracting. This marketing contract I'm doing is really good. It sort of just happened. Maybe I'll sign up to do some more contracts. It's actually sort of fun,"

I said.

Dom considered it for a moment and said, "I guess so. You've had a lot more energy lately, and it's good for you to get out of the house ... and to wake up before noon."

She was right. When I didn't have a job, I had a tendency to sleep in late and stay inside to work on my idea. It was nice to have a set schedule, even if it was only temporary. I was actually tired at night and woke up before noon. In many respects, it was less effort. I didn't have to really create anything for myself if it was all laid out nicely by a schedule. Even if I wasn't really doing much, it sure felt like I was doing more when I got out of bed before noon.

"Yeah, I've met some great people with this last contract. With all my trade show work, I probably have enough experience to be a crew leader or something."

"Sure, if you want to. I don't see why not," she said.

I thought about what it'd be like to run a crew for promotional campaigns. It was fun work, but what did I really want to do? I realized I had no idea. I'd always just done what felt right at the time. Things usually turned out well. I was at a crossroads. On one road I saw stable work and challenges. On the other road I saw absolute uncertainty and other challenges. I liked challenges, but did I want certainty? Sure, it was nice to have a schedule, but would I become bored with promotions work and wind up back at the same place in a few months? Probably.

I paid the bill and we stepped out onto the sidewalk. A cold wind was in the air. Winter was just around the corner. We zipped up our jackets. Dom reached out her hand. I met it with mine.

She said, "I think you should make a decision, one way or the other, and stick with it. It's not good to always wonder, but it's also not good to spend too much time pursuing something that isn't meant to happen. You should just try to get as close as possible to what feels right. You need to decide for yourself."

I held her close, thought for a moment, and said, "Yeah, I either need to give this red paperclip trading thing my best effort, or forget about it totally. It'll just be too much of a distraction if I'm not all in, or totally out. You know what I'm like; I can't do more than one thing at a time."

Dom looked at me, smiled, and said, "I sure know that."

I gave her a hug. Either way, Dom was with me.

We arrived back at our apartment. Dom had to wake up at 6:00 a.m. to go to work at the hospital, so she went to sleep. I sat in bed and tried to read a book. I read about ten pages and then realized I hadn't paid attention to a single word. I thought about going back for a reread, but I just folded the corner on the page and put the book down. I'd figure that out another day. I had something else to figure out tonight.

I stared up at the ceiling. What was I going to do now? I'd just completed a great work contract. An open road lay ahead. Was I going to get a job and pay the bills, or finish what I had started and try to trade from a red paperclip to a house? I didn't want to be in limbo any longer. I'd either go to bed or forge ahead. And if I was going to step up to the plate, I wanted to hit it out of the park. Nobody wants to ground out to the pitcher. I looked at my website and tried to imagine how it looked to an outsider. *I* thought it was a decent website, but when I looked at it from the eyes of a stranger, I saw something I'd never seen before: the one red paperclip website was an absolute piece of crap. It was housed on an obscure page of an old website I'd set up almost a year before. It was confusing. It was ineffective. In website terms, I'd just grounded out to the pitcher to end the inning, and left three runners stranded. I looked up at the clock.

It was 11:00 p.m.

I made the rash decision to scrap everything and build a new blog from scratch. I took all the blog entries about the trades I'd made and copied them into a new blog located at www.onered-paperclip.blogspot.com. I set it up so anyone who typed in oneredpaperclip.com would be automatically forwarded to the new blog. I created a little storyline at the top of the page that had pictures of each trade item. If somebody clicked on a picture of that trade item, it would pull up the blog entry for the story of that trade, and introduce them to each person I'd traded with. I also added my phone number and email address in a very prominent location on the website. I figured if people could understand the story of my trades better, meet some of the people I'd traded with, and easily contact me, then maybe they would be more likely to make a trade offer for my current item.

I honed down the site to the best of my ability, until I couldn't keep my eyes open anymore. I sent a link to the new site to friends, family, and a few popular sites, just for kicks. I looked at the clock on the computer screen: 4:56 a.m. Tomorrow had been today for almost five hours. Enough was enough. I didn't want to scrap the entire day. I knew I'd done my very best. Hopefully I'd find somebody who wanted to trade something for the generator. I stumbled to bed and slept like a rock.

The sun is shining somewhere right now.

It might not be over your head right now, but sooner or later, the sun will appear over the horizon, rise high in the sky, and provide warm, life-giving light. Unless, of course, you're in a cave.

Feel free to complain, we can buy earplugs.

Why complain when you can do something about it? If you think you can't do something about it, then you can't. Yes, I'm sorry to say it, but if you are certain that it is impossible, then it *is*. If you change your mind and have confidence in your idea, just remember that it might not be as easy as you expect. You might lose some sleep and have to make some tough decisions. It might not even pan out like you expect. But it *is* possible. But most of all, please think of the positives to your situation. Complainers are bad enough but earplugs aren't that comfortable, either.

Tomorrow hasn't happened yet.

But when you turn the page it might happen.

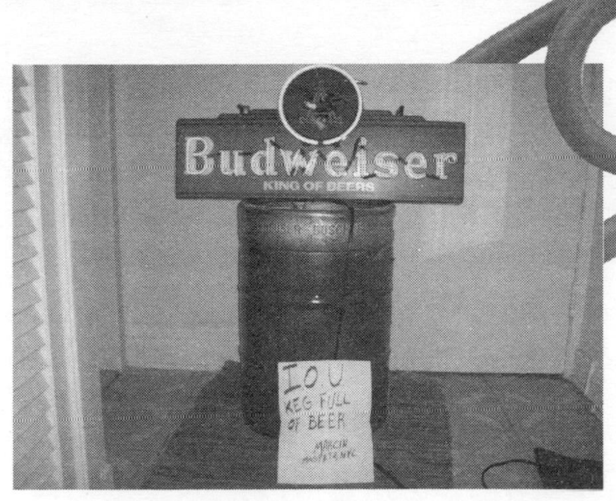

one instant party

The phone rang. Loudly. I opened my eyes wide, turned my head, and stared at it. It rang again. Sleep or phone? It was a tough choice. It rang again. Phone. I jumped out of bed and answered it.

"Hello?"

"Hey, is this Kyle?" said a perky woman's voice.

"Yep, that's me," I said.

"My name is Claire. I'm an associate producer for *The Hour* on CBC," she said.

"Cool."

The CBC is Canada's national broadcaster. Phone over sleep was a good call.

"We think your red paperclip thing is so interesting and our host, George Stroumboulopoulos, wants to interview you. Do you want to come on the show tonight and tell us about your story?"

"Um, yes. Yes, I do."

"Great. Hey, do you know your email address on the site isn't working? I think we called every K. MacDonald in the entire province of Québec trying to track you down."

"No, I didn't realize that. My website design skills are pretty hack. Did you realize that my phone number is on the front page of my website?"

"Yeah, we realized that. After we called every K. MacDonald

in the province. Most people don't put their phone number on the Internet like that, you know."

"I guess not. Hey, I've never spoken with another K. MacDonald in Québec. How are they doing?"

"Most of them were pretty confused. But other than that, quite well, I guess. Do you get a lot of weirdos calling you because your phone number is on your website?"

I let a solid five-second pause hang in the air, then said, "Well, so far, you're the only one who's called."

"Oh," she said. "Okay, I have to go to a meeting now and pitch the idea. I'll get back to you and let you know if you're on the show tonight."

"Great," I said.

"Okay, talk to you soon," she said.

"Yep, talk to you soon." I was about to hang up the phone, but I pulled it back quickly and said, "Hey, wait. Where did you hear about one red paperclip?"

"Boing Boing," she said.

"Wow," I said, and hung up the phone.

Boing Boing – a massively popular multicontributor blog about cool things. A link from Boing Boing pretty much ensured that one red paperclip would be today's watercooler fodder all over the world. Up to this point, only about thirty people a day visited my obscurely located blog with the stories of each trade. I went over to the computer to see today's visitors: thirty thousand. Today. I looked at the clock. It was 8:30 a.m. Two people per second were arriving at the site. I checked my email inbox. More than fifty emails. The phone rang again. I took a deep breath and answered.

And answered.

And answered.

The phone rang all day. Newspaper reporters, radio DJs, agents, publishers, TV producers, website developers – you name it. They all called. Dom came home from work, saw from the look on my face that I'd had quite the day, and said, "What's going on?"

"Everything. The phone hasn't stopped ringing all day," I said.

"Really? How come?"

I pointed to the website counter and my email inbox. Her eyes bulged. "Wow," she said.

Offers for the generator rolled in, but were haphazardly spread. And once again there were no offers from people in Montreal. As much as I wanted to take a spur-of-the-moment flight to Wisconsin to trade the generator for a 1989 Ford Crown Victoria, "slightly smashed (deer hit), but runs," I still couldn't justify the expense.

Claire called back a few hours later to say that something important had come up, and being a news programme, they had to cover the story. She said, "But we'll have you on the show soon. I promise."

"Sure!" I said. I was just flattered they had wanted to talk to me at all. She had no idea what kind of clothes I was wearing.

A few days later Dom and I hopped in the Corolla and drove down to New York to work another trade show for Table Shox. I definitely wasn't worried about transporting the generator in the Corolla. A red generator is *exactly* the type of thing meant to travel in a red Corolla. We stopped and filled up the car with gas. I filled up the generator as well. We got back on the highway.

"What's that smell?" Dom asked.

"Oh, I must've spilled a little bit of gas on the generator when I filled it up. Don't worry, it'll evaporate. We just need to air it out."

I rolled the window down. The car reeked of gas fumes. I thought about the TSA agent in Portland, hands on her hips, leaning back, laughing.

We made it to the hotel in Manhattan and met up with Mom and Dad, Scott, Rachel and Evian. We left the generator in the storage room on the main floor. As a result of the mention on Boing Boing, *The New York Times* had a very small mention of oneredpaperclip.com at the bottom of a wee little Internet technology article. But, boy, was Dad proud. His son was *fit to print.*

I posted on my website that I was in New York and eager to make a trade.

The next day I lined up a trade with Marcin in Queens. He had a "whole bunch of stuff" to trade: beer kegs, neon bar signs, and the like. I worked the trade show for the next two days and then set up a time to make the trade at his place on the last evening we were in town. Marcin worked early so he wanted to do it before 9:00 p.m. After we finished the final day of the trade show, we went out for dinner in Little Italy. After dinner, I walked back to the hotel to grab the generator. I pulled the claim check out of my pocket and handed it to Tony, the front desk attendant.

"I have something in the storage room," I said.

"No problem, I'll go grab it for you," he said. He walked into the storage room.

After a few minutes, he came back with a concerned look on his face and said, "I can't seem to find it, what does it look like?"

"Um, it's a box wrapped in a black garbage bag. It's kind of heavy."

"What's inside the box?" he asked.

"A gasoline-powered generator," I said.

"Oh, *that* bag. That was *your* bag?" he said.

His tone of voice made me nervous. "Yes …" I said.

"Oh."

"Oh what?" I said.

He put his hand to his chin, pondered for a moment, and said, "Let's see, how can I put this? A few nights ago the front desk clerk smelled gas fumes and dialled 911. The Fire or Police Department came in and took the bag away. You can't store a generator in a storage room, you know. It smelled like gas. Apparently people came down to the lobby from the fourth floor. They said they could smell a gas leak. People get a little bit worried about that sort of thing around here."

I understood the security hazard. I'd screwed up. Leaky generators are not meant to be stored in hotel storage rooms, especially in Lower Manhattan. That was an unspoken common understanding. I was just choked nobody had let me know about the generator's eviction. My name and room number were written on the claim check tag attached to the handle of the generator.

I stared at Tony with my mouth open and said, "But when did all this happen?"

"A few nights ago," he said.

"How come nobody told me about this? My room number was on the bag!" I said.

"I don't know. I had the night off," he said.

"But where's the generator now?"

"I don't know."

Dom was beside me. She'd arrived halfway through and heard most of the conversation. She looked at me and said, "What are you going to do now?"

I looked back at her. "I don't know."

And I didn't. The generator was gone. Even if I could track

it down I'd probably have to pay a five-hundred-dollar NYC bylaw fine for a serious offence like "causing a fire hazard" or "awakening hotel guests with something other than loud rock music". I found it a bit odd that the Fire Department would go to all the trouble of removing a suspicious device such as a leaky generator from a hotel storage room without notifying the owner. This was Lower Manhattan, after all. But then again, I find many things odd, like the colour beige. I tried to calm myself down. We'd find the generator, right? But what about the five-hundred-dollar fine I'd surely have to pay? I couldn't justify paying that much for a generator.

Tony called every fire and police station within a thirty-block radius. No luck. Nobody knew what he was talking about. But it wasn't that big a deal. I could start again from scratch, right? I could find another red paperclip, right? It wasn't the end of the world, was it?

I thought about it for a second.

No, it wasn't the end of the world, or anything close to that, but there was no way I was going to just give up like that. I'd worked hard to make those four trades from one red paperclip to one red generator. I'd *earned* that red generator. I decided I'd do everything in my power to track down that red generator and get it back.

I put my fist into the table and said, "Dom, let's go find that generator."

We left the lobby desk. I looked up at the clock on the wall. It was already 9:00 p.m. I called up Marcin and cancelled the trade. I said, "Maybe tomorrow? If we find the generator?"

"Sure, give me a call tomorrow. We'll try to meet up then," he said.

We hit the pavement and walked to every fire station we

could find. After two hours, we met up with a pair of tough-talking Fire Department sergeants sitting in a Suburban.

"A generat-*ah* huh? Whaddaya think Bobby, Ladder Twenty? Yeah, I think somebody there'll know where it is. Hop in."

We did.

"Would you like a Tootsie Pop?" Bobby said.

"Yes please!" we said.

We drove over to Ladder Twenty on Lafayette Street. The firefighters were awesome. The Tootsie Pops were delicious. They found the generator. They even had a Dalmatian.

As I picked up the generator and thanked Bobby again, he took us aside and said, "Lucky you found it tonight. Things like that have a way of 'falling off trucks', know what I mean?"

I knew exactly what he meant. Of course, without the proper straps, the generator could fall off the truck if placed on the outside during transport. And I doubt the firefighters had the proper straps for the red generator.

We thanked them for the help, and as I picked up the red generator to start the slow walk back to the hotel, Bobby said, "Hey, be careful where you store that thing from now on, will ya?"

I turned around slowly with the generator in my hands, and said, "I will. I'll put it in my car tonight. It won't be in the hotel, that's for sure."

"Good, and just because they drained all the gas from that thing don't mean it's not dangerous."

I couldn't believe what he was about to say.

Bobby added, "Yeah, it's the fumes that are dangerous."

I wrote a blog post that explained the situation briefly. We hadn't confirmed the trade with Marcin, so I wanted to have my bases covered. If he couldn't make the trade, hopefully somebody else in New York could.

"Maybe we should throw in some Tootsie Pops with the deal," I said.

Dom rolled her eyes. It'd been a long evening.

We woke up the next day and called Marcin. No answer.

I looked over at Dom and said, "After a night like last night, we can't leave the city until we trade this generator. If Marcin can't make the trade, I'm going to find somebody else. It's got to go."

"Yeah, you really need to trade that thing," she said.

We went to an internet café and I posted a series of ads in the barter section of different Craigslist pages around New York. A few curious emails rolled in over the next hour, but nobody wanted to confirm a trade.

I called Marcin again. No answer.

I posted similar Craigslist barter ads in every city on the road between New York and Montreal. Once again, a few curious emails trickled in, but nothing could be confirmed.

I called Marcin again. He answered. "Hello?" he said.

"Hey Marcin, it's Kyle, the guy with the generator. Can we make the trade today?"

"Sure, swing on by," he said.

We found our way to Marcin's place in Maspeth, about a half-hour drive from Manhattan, on Long Island. On the way, I filled the generator with gas. It just wouldn't have been right to trade it if it didn't work.

We pulled up to his place, said our hellos, and Marcin put together a great little package from his "whole bunch of stuff" as a trade offer for the red generator.

- one beer keg
- one neon Budweiser sign
- one IOU for a keg's worth of beer

Added together, it was "one instant party".

I plugged the neon Budweiser sign into the generator, pulled the cord, and the generator roared to life. Marcin switched on the sign. It lit up brightly, powered by the generator.

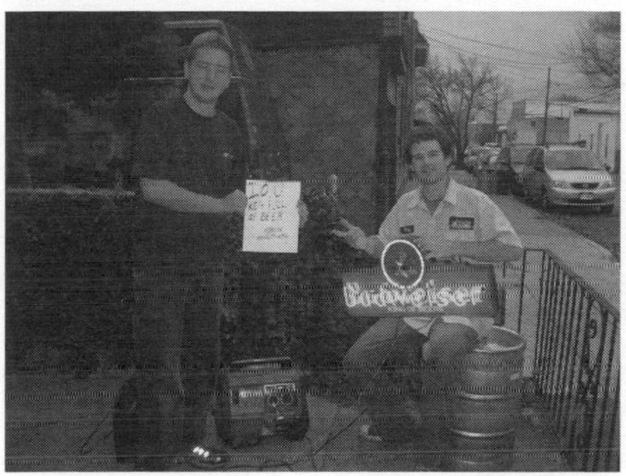

We looked at each other, shook hands and sealed the deal.

"I spend most weekends up in the country, so I'll get a lot of use out of this," Marcin said, pointing to the generator.

I was sure he'd get much more use out of it than I had.

We drove back to Montreal. I carried the assorted items that comprised "the instant party" up to our apartment and raced to the computer. I was jacked on caffeine. Super jacked. I sat down and poured my heart into a massive blog post:

This was a landmark trade, not just because of the intricacy of illuminating the neon light off of electricity from the generator or the fact that I am now in the IOU zone, but because "one instant party" has the potential for so much fun. Before anybody out there says it, I'll say it myself: the items that make up "one instant party" are probably not worth as much as one red generator:

Marcin got an awesome deal. But remember, this is not eBay. This is one red paperclip. I'm not here to sell stuff; I'm here to barter stuff – and barter is supposed to be fun. I'm not sure about you, but I'd argue that "one instant party" has a lot more potential for fun than one red generator. I'm sure Marcin will have an awesome time with his red generator – that's assured. Generators are fun too. I'm just saying that even though one red generator may have a higher cash value than one instant party, "one instant party" has more funtential. More potential for fun. And fun is priceless. By the way, I spray painted the keg red. It had to be done.

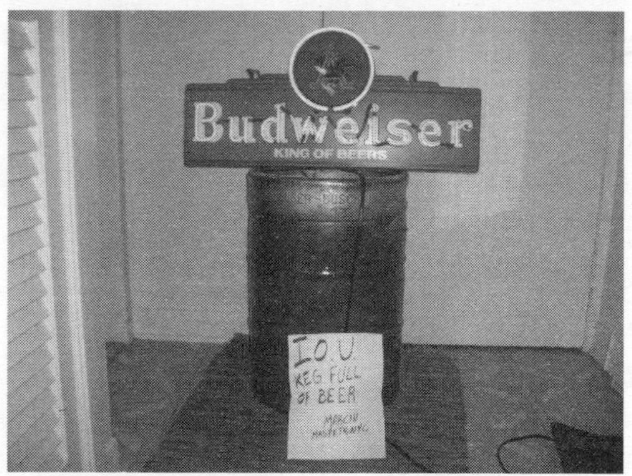

The other night after I realized the red generator was confiscated by the FDNY, I had a revelation. At this point in my mind, the generator was not an asset. It was a liability. I didn't have the money to bail out the generator. I've had loads of encouragement from many residents of blogland who want to see me complete the series of trades up to a house. I want nothing else than for this to happen. In fact, with all the help I'm getting, I feel that we're in this together and that if I don't get up to a house, I'll let you down. Bartering up to a house is going to be fun. It is going to be rad. It will rule. When I get the house, you will all be invited over. But for me to barter from one red paperclip to one house, a paradigm shift needs to occur. Definition of Paradigm Shift from somewhere Google took me: "A complete change in thinking or belief systems that allows the creation of a new condition previously thought impossible or unacceptable (e.g. the change in thinking created by Just-in-Time delivery that views inventory as a liability, not an asset)." Now I'm not saying that the whole barter from one red paperclip to a house concept needs to be Fixxed, it's just that I've come to learn that One Thing Leads to Another and that each trade I make has a massive repercussion on what future trade offers will be, whether I make a subtle random unnecessary reference to a new wave pop song from 1983 or not. What I'm saying is: I need to think outside the paperclip. With the vast amounts of funtential stored within "one instant party", the project can no longer be called just one red paperclip: This is one red paperclip 2.0

ORP 1.0 = limited to bigger or better objects, like "The World's Largest Hockey Stick"

ORP 2.0 = the same as ORP 1.0 but also includes things like "Guest host spot on *The Tonight Show*"

(Don't get me wrong here, the entire project will revert back to a pure, only object-oriented ORP 1.0 style if you or somebody else can hook up a sponsorship from a massive freight company like UHAUL or CHINA SHIPPING LINES or NASA that will pick up all freight charges plus the occasional city bylaw snafu along the way.

(I don't have room for The World's Largest Hockey Stick in my apartment, but I will make some if it comes up for trade.)

I need to start trading liquid assets. Things that have the potential to be retraded quickly. Things that will sell themselves.

Things that will not get confiscated by the FDNY. Things like beer. Okay, bad example, but I hope you get my point. What I'm trying to say is that I want to spend more time actually trading things and less time improving them and searching for trade offers. It took 53 days to trade the generator. 53 days is WAY too long. 53 days is not fun, 53 days is boring. 53 days is so one red paperclip 1.0

I appreciate the dozens of offers for vehicles that only need a few new parts to get them back on the road – parts like "left side rear-view mirror" or "shifter knob" or "entire new drive train and frame-straightening" – but what you need to understand is, I don't have any tools. I've got a hammer, some scissors, a Swiss Army knife and a few rolls of duct tape. Unless you can provide the garage, the labour and the parts to fix the vehicle, then a handful of rolls of duct tape isn't going to make the vehicle any easier for me to trade for something else. (If you have an original General Lee, in any condition, please disregard this paragraph) I'm really excited about this. This is such a big step in the right direction – the direction of awesome.

P.S. Lessons learned from "one red generator":

- Some things are not meant to fly – like a gasoline-powered electrical generator.
- Some things are not meant to be stored in hotel storage rooms – like a gasoline-powered electrical generator.
- Some things are not easy to barter in New York City when New York City is not suffering from a crippling blackout – like a gasoline-powered electrical generator.
- Funtential is now a real word.
- Furiousity is not a real word. Yet.

To encourage an early arrival of awesome, I set a deadline for offers on one instant party. December 1. Nothing happens without a deadline. I added a disclaimer to the deadline that I would wait until 11:59 p.m. on November 30 to make my decision, unless I received an offer I couldn't refuse.

On Thursday a small article about oneredpaperclip.com ran in a column called Networthy in *The Mirror*, a free weekly entertainment newspaper in Montreal. We went down to the nearest newsstand and picked up a copy. There it was, an article about one redpaperclip.com. In the paper. Right above a short blurb about a *sensationally popular* blog called coreyhartdrivesafiero.blogspot.com. Wow. Now I was in the *big leagues.*

The horse in my pocket whinnied happily. I pulled it out, flipped it open, and said, "Hello?"

A man's voice said, "Hey Kyle, I just read about your website in *The Mirror*, I'd really like to write an article about it for my newspaper."

"Sure, sounds good to me! When do you want to meet?" I said.

"Does *now* work for you?"

"Yes. *Now* works. *Now* is perfect," I said

We arranged to meet at our apartment.

"Great, I'll see you soon," he said.

"Sorry, I didn't catch your name," I said.

"Patrick Lagacé," he said.

"And your newspaper?" I said.

"*Le Journal de Montreal.*"

Wow. *Le Journal de Montreal.* The biggest newspaper in Québec. This was a very good phone call.

"Who was that?" Dom asked.

"A guy from *Le Journal de Montreal.* He wants to do a story about one red paperclip," I said.

"What guy?" Dom asked.

"Um, he said his name was Patrick something."

"Patrick Lagacé?" she said.

"Yeah, I think so. Something like that."

"If that's him, this is very good. He's a very good reporter. You know this guy, remember? The guy who hitchhiked to cover the election?"

"That's him?" I said. "The guy who was on TV and talked about snowmobiles?"

"*Oui*," said Dom.

Wow. I was really excited to meet Patrick. He was a bit of a big deal. The year before he'd hitchhiked across Canada to cover the national election for *Le Journal*. His articles were about the people who gave him rides, and their thoughts on the upcoming election. I'd also seen him in a very heated debate on a Québecois TV programme. The show was called *110%* and the topic was "Snowmobiles: Public Nuisance or Beneficial Activity?" Patrick was assigned to argue that they were a nuisance. Only in Québec can a major TV network have an hour-long debate about snowmobiles. In primetime. Patrick was the kind of reporter I really admired. A true reporter. The kind of guy who goes right to the source.

In true Lagacian fashion, Patrick came right to the source. Our apartment. He even brought a real journalist's notebook. He flipped open the notebook and fired away.

"Do you have a deadline for when you want to trade up to a house?" he said.

I thought about it for a second. "I don't have a deadline, but I'd like to trade from one red paperclip to a house in one year. I started on July 12 of this year, so I'd like to finish by July 12 next year. But, of course, that's off the record. Please don't put that in the article. It's not like I'm really serious about it or anything, just that it'd be fun to do it in one year. "

Patrick nodded. He was a cool guy. He'd keep it out of his article.

"When will the article run in *Le Journal*?" I asked.

"Tomorrow for sure."

"Super," I said.

Some friends came over for dinner that evening and we told them all about it. They were really excited. I figured Patrick's article would be a small human interest story in the back, probably adjacent to the cat-stuck-in-a-tree offbeat news section. But Dom's friend Marie-Eve finished her mouthful of spaghetti and said, "No way. Front page, for sure."

We all laughed. Marie-Eve was hilarious. The front page. Right.

The next morning I slept in. The phone rang. It was Marie-Eve. She asked, "Did you see *Le Journal* yet?"

"No, not yet," I said.

She was surprised, "No?! Go buy one now."

I didn't need to know more. "Okay, I will."

My picture was on the front page of *Le Journal de Montreal*. In colour. I flipped to the article. It took up nearly an entire page, and was directly adjacent to an article about snowmobiles. Perfect. I read the article. My mouth dropped. I couldn't believe it! He said that I was trying to trade up to a house by July 12. Patrick had lied. It was public knowledge now. I just had to bite my lip and deal with it. People would believe Patrick. He'd used a real journalist's notebook. It was practically court ledger. And by now, maybe even *law*.

I looked at the calendar. It was November 25. I did some quick finger math. December, January, February, March, April, May, June, July. Middle finger right hand. Eight months. And less than half of July. If I was going to keep my word, or more accurately *Patrick's* word, I had to trade up to a house in seven and a half months.

For the rest of the day, most of Dom's friends and relatives called. Apparently every radio station in Quebec was talking about the guy with "le trombone rouge".

The offers rolled in.

*****I'd gladly trade you a gas-powered snowblower, a milk can (the kind they used to fill up from the farm), and a box of 8 52-in-1 NES cartridges with convertors (because they're the Japanese Famicom type) for your Instant Party. How about it?
Cheers, MC

*****I would like to offer one Mystery Box in trade for the Instant Party.

*****16 Pack of Charmin Toilet Paper. White toilet paper is going to be very handy after the Instant Party, especially if it's filled with Bud.

*****Hi Kyle!
I really hope that I will be the first Quebecer to do a trade with you. Because the winter is on his way, I am offering you 4 winter tyres for the Budweiser sign. They are like brand new (only a winter and a half). If it doesn't work, let me congratulate you for your project and I really hope that you will achieve your dream.
Yours truly, Guy

*****Sympa ton histoire! Je t'offre un ballon de soccer officiel de la Ligue de soccer élite du Québec. Good Luck!
Marc-André Lord Commissaire Ligue de Soccer Élite du Québec

*****Okay jai quelques choix pour toi ... Une collection de cartes (d'hockey) O-Pee-Chee 2003 les amateur en raffole elle sont placée pas fiche numeroté comprend la carte de mario lemieux lors de sa premiere saison dans la ligne national de hockey (ça vaut assez cher merci!) ou une vielle collection de 45 tour qui valle po mal chere mais je te conseil les cartes d'hockey tu risque de faire plus furreur avec! N'échange pas se baril et cette ensaigne avec neon sans m'avoir dit si t'es d'accord pcq sinon je vais regarder! Good luck!
Pierrot

By Friday afternoon, the temperatures had dropped significantly. A layer of snow covered the ground. The air was cold, but the offers were red hot. I checked my email.

***** Bonjour Kyle
Nous avons lu votre histoire dans le journal de Montréal ce matin.
Nous travaillons à la station de radio 98.5FM de Montréal.
Notre animateur-vedette Michel Barrette a une proposition d'échange pour vous:
Sa motoneige Bombardier Mac 1 1991, remise à neuf.
Pour tous les québécois, elle a une valeur ajoutée puisqu'elle a appartenu à un célèbre humoriste et comédien de chez nous. Pensez-y!! ...
Bien à vous
Josée Bournival

Another offer in French. My eyes glazed over and I skimmed it in confusion. But I went back and looked at it again. There was something good in there. I looked at it hard. From what I could gather, a guy named Michel had just made an offer of a snowmobile. A snowmobile! A snowmobile was perfect. The type of offer I couldn't refuse. Especially at the beginning of winter. Especially in Québec. Québec and snowmobiles are like, well, Québec and snowmobiles. One simply cannot exist without the other. I was excited. I yelled to the other room, "Dom, come check this out!"

I pointed at the screen and watched Dom read. She mouthed the words semi-silently. She got to the fourth line and said, "Michel Barrette?! You got an offer from Michel Barrette?!"

"Yeah, apparently. Who's Michel Barrette?" I said.

"What do you mean?" she said.

I gave her a blank look and shrugged my shoulders.

She looked at me with disbelief. "You don't know who is Michel Barrette? He's very famous here in Québec. He's a comedian. He has a TV show. He does movies. *Everybody* knows Michel Barrette."

"But it says here he's a radio host or something?" I said.

"Yes. He hosts a radio show, *now*. Trust me, everyone knows this guy."

This was definitely the kind of offer I couldn't refuse. Michel would definitely help spread the word of my plan. After all, he was Michel Barrette. *The* Michel Barrette.

We checked the website for the radio station. There was a picture of a guy on the website. Dom pointed to the picture and said, "*That's* Michel Barrette." The show listings indicated that Michel was on air at the moment.

We flicked on the radio and tuned in to his station. A voice came from the speaker. Dom pointed at the radio, "And *that's* his voice."

I waited for a commercial break, then called the producer, Josée. I introduced myself and was met with a big "*Mais oui*!" on the other end of the line. I let her know that I was very eager to make a trade with Michel. She said perfect. Since it was Friday afternoon, she'd tell Michel and they'd arrange the trade for next week. Click. We listened to the radio. After the commercial break, they came back and started talking about the guy with *le trombone rouge*. I understood most of what they said, but needed a little help with the exact details. I looked at Dom, "What did they say, *exactly*?"

"They just told all of Québec that next week you and Michel Barrette are going to make a trade."

"Perfect. I've got less than eight months to get to that house!"

If you really want to, you will.

How far will you go to make it happen? If you really, truly want to see it happen, you can find a way. Even if your way gets confiscated by the Fire Department.

The water cooler is the strongest marketing device ever invented.

After the experience with the mention of one red paperclip on Boing Boing, I realized that many people talk to each other all the time about things they find interesting. People speak about things they find interesting in the form of words, from their mouths. Other people listen to those words, and if they find them interesting, they go somewhere else and tell other people the same words about the same things. And so on. It's sort of like a phenomenon involving mouths and words. If I had to invent a term to describe this phenomenon of mouths and of words, I think I'd describe it as, a *word-of-mouth phenomenon*. Yes. Word-of-mouth. I think that has a nice ring to it.

What's your funtential?

How are you going to maximize your potential for fun? Think of things you enjoy and things other people enjoy. Try to get as close to the things you enjoy as possible and encourage others to get as close to the things they enjoy as possible as well. The closer everyone is to the things they enjoy, the easier it is for people to live up to their funtential.

one famous snowmobile

I preempted the December 1 deadline. Yanked the tablecloth right off the table and left the wine glasses standing. It had to be done. Michel Barrette's snowmobile was the kind of trade offer I couldn't refuse. After all, he was *the* Michel Barrette.

The phone rang. It was Claire from *The Hour*. She said, "Want to come on the show Monday and talk to George about your trading adventure?"

"Sure!" I said.

On Monday I was excited. And nervous. I'd never appeared nationwide on live TV before. Just the sound of it was impressive. *Nationwide*. The best part about being nationwide in Canada is that Canada is a really wide country. It just wouldn't be the same to appear nationwide on TV in a skinny country like Portugal or Chile. Not at all.

I was interviewed by George Stroumboulopoulos, Canada's reigning champ for news anchor with the longest last name and most body piercings.

It was a live satellite interview. George was in Toronto; I was in Montreal. George gave a rundown of the trades I'd made, and there were cool graphics for each trade. It was an amazing experience. I'd never had graphics before.

George asked me, quite succinctly, "Is there anywhere you won't go, for this deal?"

Without hesitation, I responded firmly, "I will go anywhere in the world except for Yahk, British Columbia."

George laughed, and asked, "Why's that?"

"Well, I need to say I won't go somewhere, and Yahk seems like a great place not to go," I said.

"Well, Baghdad is another option you could take ..." he said.

"Well, I've never been to Baghdad, but I have been to Yahk. And I can tell you, it's not the greatest place to trade things," I said.

"Fair enough, that's cool," he said.

Then I went home to bed. It was a Monday, after all.

The next morning there was something about an orange banana, but that's a story for later.

After the nationwide exposure for my quest, I received calls from more Canadian nationwide news programmes. Then CNN called. They wanted in on the story too. I was really excited. CNN meant nationwide broadcast in the U.S. of A. Like Canada, the United States is a really *wide* country. If you include places like Alaska, Hawaii and Guam, the USA is *arguably* wider than Canada. With that in mind, I was certain that an appearance on nationwide TV in the States was going to be lots of fun.

On the day of the trade I had to cut short the interviews in our apartment with two camera crews from Canadian national newscasts because I was running late for a satellite interview with CNN. We booted the TV crews from our apartment, grabbed the items that made up "one instant party", and ran to the TV studio in downtown Montreal for the CNN interview. It has hectic.

Up to this point, the only video of the project was the one that Dom shot, the low-res, one-take clip of Marcin and me swapping the generator for the instant party. But all these news programmes had really good cameras, and that meant good footage. And when it comes to cameras, CNN pretty much has the best *cameras* around, so you know they pretty much broadcast the best news.

The CNN interview was fun. I talked to Kyra Phillips for a few minutes about my plan to trade from a red paperclip to a house. The neon Budweiser sign sat beside me. I showed her the IOU. We smiled and were excited about what was going to happen next.

Dom and I drove down to the CKOI radio station building where Michel Barrette worked. There were a few camera crews hanging out front. It was a cold day. A foot of snow was on the ground. It was the perfect day to trade a snowmobile. By now, news of the trade with *the* Michel Barrette had spread around Québec and the local Montreal newscasts were "on it" with their "action news" vans and all.

We hopped out of the red Corolla and said hi to everybody. I pulled the "instant party" kit from the car and placed it on the curb. A guy with sunglasses came around the corner and walked in our direction. I stepped to one side of the sidewalk to let him pass. He came near us and hesitated. A large grin broke across his face. "The paperclip guy!" he said.

I smiled politely and thought to myself, "Did this guy just watch CNN or something?" He took off his sunglasses. It was Michel Barrette. We shook hands and smiled at each other. He reached into his pocket and pulled out a small paper bag. He extended his hand toward me, looked right into my eyes, and said, "Do you want a cookie?"

I said thanks and bit into the cookie. It was delicious. Cookies are like that.

Michel opened up the back of a giant semi truck he'd arranged to transport the snowmobile down from northern Québec. We climbed in and scoped out the snowmobile.

Michel grabbed the starter cord. It fired on the first pull. He revved the engine and looked at me with a big grin. The TV cameras rolled. He revved it up real good and checked a few gauges. He hopped off and gestured for me to hop on. I got on and grabbed the handlebars. Just as I was about to rev it up and generally make a lot of noise and exhaust fumes for the TV cameras, Michel grabbed my hand and stared right at me. "Don't rev it too high. It will take off and you'll go right through the front wall of this truck."

I thought about it for a moment. That's not the kind of thing I'd ever imagined doing. Smashing through the front end of a tractor trailer. On national TV. I briefly considered going for it. After all, the footage would be amazing, but I thought about what Mom would say, and reconsidered. I couldn't smash through the front of the truck. I didn't have my helmet on. I carefully revved it up just enough to make a lot of noise and blow some exhaust out the back of the trailer for the camera guys. They ate it up. Camera guys are like that.

Michel and I did the obligatory "handshake" picture, and I walked over to Dom with a massive grin plastered across my face.

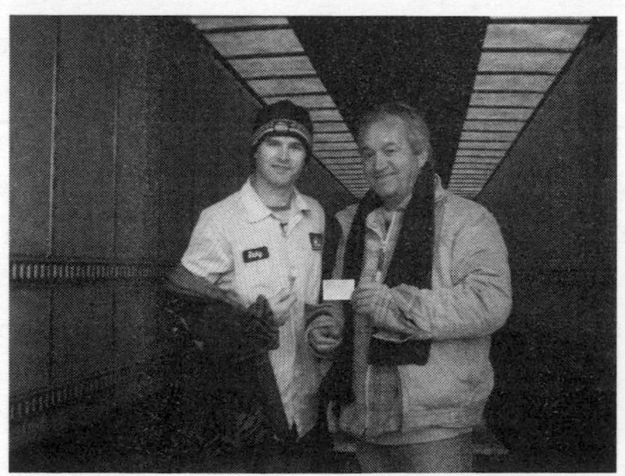

This was it. A snowmobile. In only a few trades I'd managed to parlay one red paperclip into a snowmobile. We stood inside the tractor trailer, several feet off the ground and looked out the back into the distance. Dom was Kate Winslet and I was Leonardo DiCaprio. We were at the front of the *Titanic* with the wind in our face and an endless expanse of open ocean in front of us. Anything was possible. Nothing could go wrong.

I felt a hand on my shoulder and turned around. Michel Barrette pointed at the snowmobile, "So Mister Paperclip, the driver of this truck wants to know where he can drop off your snowmobile."

I looked over at Dom. She gave me "the look".

Uh oh. I hadn't thought of this. I always assumed the snowmobile would stay at the radio station until I figured out my next trade. What should I tell him? I was in a pickle. I hate being in pickles. Actually, I can honestly say that pickles are my least favourite food. Definitely the most overrated gherkin. I thought hard. Our apartment was tiny and it was on the third floor, so that was out. My buddy Mathieu was at work, and it'd be pretty cheeky to drop it off at his house, which actually happened to be his parents' house. I could definitely make it up to him with vast amounts of beer at a later date, but I'd just gone and traded away my IOU for a full keg of beer.

Dom shook her head, gave me another "look", and said, "Nice one. I told you, you should find a place for that snowmobile. What were you thinking? That it would just find a place all by itself?"

I wanted to say yes, because that's exactly what I thought. I really did think it would work itself out.

I frantically thought about where I could store the now-famous snowmobile. Then it hit me: Justin. I looked at Dom, who was still all about the "look", and said, "What about Justin? He said I could probably keep it in his garage for a while."

She looked back at me. "The look" became "the voice'. "What? You can't just send it over there now. You need to give him notice. You can't just ask him at the last minute, just like that."

But I couldn't give Justin notice. I only had the last minute. Just like that.

Anyhow, Justin was the kind of guy who'd understand. When we'd met a few years previously at a hostel in Australia, he was fresh off the plane from Québec and hardly spoke a word of English. It must've been incredibly difficult for him. The Aussies gave him the gears because he didn't speak English. He couldn't even understand simple English phrases like, "How ye goin mate? Yeh, toss the slab of VB in the ute. That sheila you were just talking to's got a few roos loose in the top paddock but I reckon you can get a quick root in before you head down to Melly Saturday arvo."

He asked me quite often what the Aussies were talking about, and I filled him in. Or lied and made things up because I didn't understand. He and I had laughed about it then. He must've felt so humble, not knowing what *ute* or *sheila* or *slab of VB* or *arvo* or *Melly* meant. Sheesh. He must've felt like a *total* moron.

But now was my turn to feel like a moron. I pulled out my phone and dialled Justin. He answered right away. Just like that.

"Hello?" he said.

I looked up. Two TV cameras were in my face. The red lights were on. I swallowed, then went for it. "Hey Justin, remember how you said I might be able to keep the snowmobile at your place?"

"Yeah ..." he said.

"Well, um, I kinda just found out I need to find a place to keep it for a while."

Justin laughed. He couldn't see the cameras, and I didn't exactly give him a full description of my situation, but I'm sure he heard it in my voice. It was such sweet revenge for all the times we'd laughed at him in Australia.

"Is it cool if it comes to your place?" I asked, with hope in my eyes, and voice.

He laughed again, and said, "Sure man. I'll give you the address."

"Thanks."

The camera guys ate it up. Camera guys are like that.

I gave Justin's address to the truck drivers. We said goodbye to the camera guys and reporters. Then, Michel, Dom and I lugged the instant party into the radio station. We made our way to a room filled with people who milled about, and shook many hands. There were no TV cameras here. It's funny how a room filled with lots of people who ask you rapid-fire questions in French can be a relaxing stress-free oasis after a day spent in front of multiple TV cameras. I could make the most embarrassing phone call of all time and it wouldn't be replayed on national TV. I considered making a really embarrassing phone call, just for kicks. Being able to make unlimited amounts of embarrassing phone calls without national TV coverage was always something I'd taken for granted. It's funny how things change when you go on national TV.

Michel and I sat in the studio and talked on his radio show about my plan to trade up to a house. I'd never spoken on the radio in French before. I was nervous. I managed to hold my own in French, and even convinced Dom to get in on the conversation. She was nervous too, seeing how all her friends and family were listening.

Going on the radio in French was a big end to a big day. When I first came to Québec a few years before, I hardly spoke a word of French. Learning French was the hardest, most humbling experience of my entire life. Way harder than that silly little last-minute phone call to Justin. In the years previous to arriving in Québec, I'd worked outside as a roughneck on oil rigs at forty below, and that was tough, but nothing compares to sitting at the dinner table with your girlfriend's family, totally oblivious to the real life in front of your eyes. It's amazing how we English-first-languagers have it. We expect everybody to understand us wherever we go, and for the most part, they do. It's amazing when the coin is flipped and you find yourself as an outsider to a culture. Especially in your own country.

I didn't need to speak French on the radio to prove that I was "down" with Québec, and I had no illusions of suddenly being Québecois or something. (My accent assured that.) But when I spoke to Michel on the radio in French, with all of Dom's family listening, I felt like I'd finally bridged the gap. At the very least I had a little bit of Quebecois street cred. I'd chilled with Michel Barrette. *The* Michel Barrette.

Michel planned to give "the instant party" to his buddy as a gift. He'd originally planned to give the same guy the snowmobile he'd traded me. He thought it'd be way more fun to give his buddy a full keg of beer, a Budweiser sign, and then throw in about thirty additional cases of bonus beer, just for kicks. His buddy might be choked at first but figured he'd get over it after a handful of beers. After another handful he'd probably think Michel was a genius. One thing was certain, I definitely thought Michel Barrette was a genius. A genius and a really cool guy.

Michel looked over at me and said, "Who do you think you'll trade the snowmobile with?"

I smiled, thought about an orange banana-flavoured secret. "I have some really good offers, but nothing's certain yet. I think I'll decide very soon. I have a good idea of what it'll be," I said, again with a smirk on my face.

"Great, let us know when you make your decision!" he said.

"I will," I said.

Dom and I waved goodbye and headed home.

So now that I've hyped it enough, the orange banana thing: I'd kept something secret since the morning after my appearance on *The Hour*. The morning after *The Hour*, I'd received an amazing offer for the snowmobile, but it wasn't a confirmed offer. When Dom and I arrived home after hanging out with Michel, I checked my email. The offer was confirmed. I punched the air and said "Yes!"

I walked into the kitchen and said to Dom, "Yes."

"Yes, what?" she said.

"Jeff said, 'Green light'. The offer is official," I said.

"Jeff who?" she said.

"Orange Banana Jeff," I said.

"Ah, good," she said.

Setting: Kyle and Dom's apartment. Morning after Kyle's interview with George Stroumboulopoulos. Early morning. Phone rings. Kyle ponders whether to answer it or sleep in. Phone rings again. Kyle answers the phone.

Kyle: Hello.

Jeff: Hello, is Kyle there?

Kyle: (Clears throat) Yup. That's me.

Jeff: Hey, Kyle, how's it going?

Kyle: Good. You?

Jeff: Great. Let me introduce myself, it's not like this is a movie script and you know who I am right? My name is Jeff Cooper and I work for a magazine in Cranbrook, British Columbia, called *SnoRiders West*. We're conveniently located forty-five minutes from Yahk.

Kyle: Nice! I guess you saw *The Hour* last night.

Jeff: Actually I didn't. But a co-worker of mine, Kerry, told me all about it.

Kyle: Cool.

Jeff: Well, we've been throwing some ideas around here at the office. We want to make you an offer for your snowmobile.

Kyle: Really? What's your offer?

Jeff: We want to offer you a trip to Yahk.

Jeff is serious. He offers return airfare for two people from anywhere in North America to Cranbrook, a day of skiing, meals, and a snowmobile trip to Yahk. This is big news. A trip to Yahk. Kyle agrees with Jeff that this is an amazing offer. The funtential *of a trip to Yahk is off the charts.*

Kyle: This is perfect.

Jeff: But there's a catch.

Kyle: What's that?

Jeff: Well, actually there are two catches. The first catch is that we have to clear this with the boss.

Kyle: What's the second catch?

Jeff: The second catch is, you must make the trade in Yahk.

Kyle breaks fourth wall and looks directly at camera. His eyes bug out and he makes an astonished face. Screen pauses at moment of most astonishment. Cue appropriate about-to-cut-to-a-commercial music.

You are reading this right now.

It happened. For real. And it'll happen again. Somewhere. Somehow. But different. Will it happen to you?

Look over the fence.

The grass isn't necessarily greener on the other side, but maybe it is. Listen to the advice of other people, but remember that we all see colour differently. What may be less green to someone else might be greener to you.

one trip to Yahk

But how could I make a trade in Yahk? I had said I'd go anywhere in the world to make a trade, *except* Yahk. It wasn't a joke, I was serious. Yeah, I'd said it. And I'd said it on TV. Nationwide.

After my movie-style Orange Banana flashback, where I broke "the fourth wall" to look into the camera, I came back to my senses, smiled into the phone and said, "It's all about Yahk."

"Yes, exactly. It's all about Yahk," said Jeff.

I agreed on principle to the trade for the trip to Yahk right there on the spot, but didn't get confirmation that it was an official offer until a few days later when I checked my email, punched the air and said "Yes!" after the trade with Michel Barrette. Thus the reason for the fun code-name secretiveness.

So I had a trip to Yahk. I just had to find a way to make the trade in Yahk and not go back on my word about not making a trade in Yahk. I, of course, also had no idea how I'd get the snowmobile from Montreal to Yahk, a distance of three thousand miles, but I figured that was another thing that'd work itself out.

I knew where I wanted to go, I just had no idea how I was going to get there.

I was lucidly confused.

Whatever that means.

Over the past week, many people asked why I wouldn't make a trade in Yahk, of all places. *Did you have something up your sleeve? Do you know something we don't know about?* For my interview with George Stroumboulopoulos on *The Hour*, I'd said "Yahk, British Columbia" as a total lark. Yahk is just a fun word to say. What rhymes with *back, crack* and *snack,* and is an obscure small town nobody's heard of? *Yahk!*

But I'd been to Yahk before. That's why I'd said it.

On a family trip, in our old white Chevy van, in British Columbia when I was a kid, Dad had pointed out Yahk on the tattered 1986 Rand McNally British Columbia map. "How about this one, Yahk!" he said with a smile on his face. He'd grown up in Nelson, a few towns over from Yahk. For all intents and purposes, he was pretty big on Yahk. I'd stared at that old map for countless hours on family trips over the years and my eyes always landed on Yahk. If there was a random town on the face of the earth more overdue for exposure than Warren, Australia, or Puyallup, Washington, it was Yahk.

So I'd said *Yahk* for fun. I didn't have a personal vendetta against Yahk or the citizens of Yahk, it's just a lot more fun to say you *won't* go somewhere really obscure, than say you'll go *anywhere*. Anywhere is boring. Anywhere is clichéd. Anywhere is not Yahk. I never imagined I'd actually get a trade offer from Yahk, but that kind of thinking had gotten me in my current pickle. I might be a lot of things, but a liar is not one of them. But since I said I wouldn't make a trade in Yahk, I'd lose *all* the credibility I'd built over the years if I did just that. *All* of it.

I would have to make some crafty moves to get out of this one unscathed. My reputation was at stake here. I thought long and hard, went for a run, did a little soul-searching, and realized something: I really didn't like the term *soul-searching*. That, and there was a way to trade with Jeff without being a liar: *All* I had to do was tell a lie.

I wrote a message to the citizens of Yahk and put it on my website:

Dear Citizens of Yahk,
On December 5th, CBC anchorman and body piercing fanatic George Stroumboulopoulos put me on the spot on live TV and asked if there was anyplace I would not go to make a trade. I told him that I would go anywhere on Earth to make a trade, except Yahk, B.C. Don't get mad at me for this, get mad at George Stroumboulopoulos. Why? I'll let you in on a little secret – I think he hypnotized me. Yes, I think George Stroumboulopoulos hypnotized me on live TV with a double whammy of his extremely long, impossible-to-remember-how-to-spell last name and abundant body piercings. He forced me to say that I would not go to Yahk to make a trade. I've been to Yahk before. Yahk seems like a very nice place. I'm sure you're a nice person too, it's just that George Stroumboulopoulos forced me to announce an official trade embargo with your town. I hope you can live with the stigma of being the only place on Earth I cannot go to make a trade. We can still be friends, just not trading partners. Maybe the citizens of Yahk should boycott George Stroumboulopoulos in retaliation for his heavy-handed hypnotic prowess – seems like the most logical thing to me. Actually, I think somebody should start a petition to get George Stroumboulopoulos to do a live broadcast of **The Hour** on CBC from Yahk to apologize for his evil ways. Yes, if there's anybody out there who knows how to organize an online petition, can you set it up and forward me the link? Thanks in advance – this is definitely a step in the right direction. Thank you for your understanding.
Kyle

Twenty minutes later, I got an email from a fellow named Brent.

Hey Kyle,
Just read your last blog post. Here's your petition:

To: George Stroumboulopoulos, CBC (Canadian Broadcasting Corporation)
We citizens of Yahk, British Columbia, Canada, and by association, all residents of planet Earth who do not live in Yahk hereby challenge George Stroumboulopoulos to do a remote broadcast of **The Hour** on CBC live from Yahk when Kyle MacDonald of www.oneredpaperclip.com will be present to "not make a trade". If George Stroumboulopoulos makes the broadcast from Yahk, the hypnotic spell he placed on Kyle MacDonald on live TV will be reversed and future trades for the one red paperclip project will finally be allowed to take place in Yahk.
Sincerely, The Undersigned.

I posted a link to the petition on the website. By the time I went to bed there were already a few signatures. By the next day even more people had put their names on the petition. I thought to myself, *this might actually work!* Anything is possible, right?

I wrote a blog post addressed to all potential traders for the trip to Yahk:

POTENTIAL TRADERS
I said on international TV that I'd go anywhere in the world to make a trade except Yahk, British Columbia, Canada, and I'm not a liar, so we'll have to make the actual trade for your item outside of Yahk. I hope you understand. Thanks Jeff, for putting this together. This goes out to everybody out there in Internet Land: I can't wait to see your offer for "one trip to Yahk" – I can't wait

to not make a trade with you in Yahk. Unless George Stroumboulopoulos reverses the hypnotic spell. Yes, the hypnotic spell unleashed on yours truly by Strombo himself. A combination of clever tactics, fast-talking, and an abundance of facial piercing later, and George had me under a spell.

The "controversy" caused quite a stir in Yahk. Penny A. P. Anderson from the Yahk-Kingsgate historical society, and a self-described Yahktivist, posted the petition on the Yahk-Kingsgate community website and warned George Stroumboulopoulos that his hypnotic powers would have no effect on the citizens of Yahk. Penny sent me an email:

"Keep watching ... someone picked the right community!"

I forwarded all of this to Claire at *The Hour*. She returned my email right away:

To: Kyle MacDonald
Subject: Re: George'll wanta see this
Message: Make sure you watch the show tonight!

Dom and I didn't have cable so we went over to her sister Marie-Lou's place and commandeered her TV. I was nervous about Claire's email: *"Make sure you watch the show tonight!"* It implied that something special might happen. That, or *The Hour* had a remarkably small marketing budget and had resorted to a direct email campaign. George came on the show and described his situation to the nation. He explained how I'd made the accusation that he'd hypnotized me. I didn't accuse him of hypnotizing me. Everyone knew it was true. Him with his power of hypnosis and all. He gave the rundown of the petition and said that he was caught in the middle of "some sort of bizarro love triangle". George said that he and everyone at *The Hour* would watch the petition and see how it went. George also added, "Unlike Kyle, I would definitely like to spend some time in Yahk, British Columbia."

This made me even more nervous, but also excited. I fully expected George to shoot down the idea. If he did, at least we'd know he had a malicious vendetta against all citizens of Yahk and I'd look like a hero. Now *I* was the villain. We had to wait and see how the petition went. And like Tom Petty says, the waiting is the hardest part.

Despite the uncertainty over the trading locale, trade offers for Yahk arrived in my email inbox:

*******I own the Kootenay Country Comfort Inn in Cranbrook BC. I will trade you 60 nights of accommodation in my motel that can be used during the ski season. These rooms come with continental breakfast.**

*******Hey, Kyle**
My name is Martin and I live in the area of Sudbury Ont. All I have to offer you at this time for your trip to Yahk is a 1994 Ford Thunderbird it has about 370,000 km but still runs quite well and the brakes and shock, struts & springs were replaced within the last ½ yrs a new rack&pinion too. Needs a good home. If you're interested in more details you could call me at (705) 855 XXXX or email if you're not. Thanks for your time and good luck hope this is what you're looking for. I love winter and the Yahk area of B.C. skied fernie once ;-)

*******I have been keeping up with your story via your blog. Not**

making much mainstream press down in South Carolina. I thought I would make trade offer. The trip for the following: My boat named Dangeresque 2 "This time it's not Dangersque 1" 1971 Fabuglas Tri-Hull, 1984 Evinrude 70HP Outboard, Bimini Top, Seating for 6, Tube, Tow Rope for Tubing, 6 Fishing Rod Holders, Fish Finder, Dual 6 Gallon Gas Tanks, Trailer. It runs great and has caught many fish.

And dozens more.

Around Christmas, we were really busy with "holiday" stuff, like family dinners, Yuletide cheer, and a move to a different apartment in the middle of winter. There's really nothing that brings out joy in people like lifting boxes full of heavy objects and placing them in a different place. That, and washing a previous tenant's bathtub scum. We moved in to the new place with our friends Mathieu and Marie-Claude. It was a good move, the ceilings in the new place were higher, and I had my own office so I wouldn't keep Dom up all night with my "drop-the-clutch-at-midnight" work habits.

By the time we were all moved in, almost one thousand people had signed the petition. Not too shabby for a petition based on an outlandish claim and an unlikely-to-come-true scenario. Not bad at all. But it didn't really matter if *The Hour* came to Yahk or not. I'd found a loophole. I could go to Yahk without being a liar!

Jeff Cooper sent me some photos of himself in Yahk and I discovered a technicality. There was a sign in Yahk that read: "YAHK – UNINCORPORATED". If Yahk wasn't incorporated as a city or town or village or hamlet, then there was a massive gray area as to where Yahk actually began and ended. I could theoretically say that I'm in Yahk right now, and so can you. Yahk is nowhere and everywhere at once. It's crazy like that. I liked the loophole. It meant I was free to go to Yahk and make the trade, because, officially, Yahk didn't really exist. Now, admittedly this was a major cop-out and optimism stretched to its theoretical limit (and creepiness), but nevertheless, a loophole. And a way to save *all* the credibility I'd built over the years. I thought about my loophole proudly. It's not everyday you discover a loophole.

But, really, I wanted to coerce George Stroumboulopoulos and *The Hour* to go to Yahk. Loopholes are fun, but not nearly as fun as watching wide-scale public opinion force a national news broadcast to travel across the continent to create live television on the back of an outlandish claim about hypnosis. That kind of thing's way more fun than a loophole any day of the week.

I spoke with Penny A. P. Anderson. She said everything was in full effect at her end. The community had met and decided that the best course of action would be to keep at the petition and continue to send emails to everyone at *The Hour*. She said how some people had made videos of local children asking George why he didn't want to go to Yahk.

The signatures continued to roll in for the petition. When the petition hit about one-thousand two-hundred signatures, I received an email from Claire at *The Hour*. I opened it with hope in my eyes. Claire had big news. They'd followed the petition's progress and made a decision: the trip to Yahk was on. *The Hour* was going to do a show live from Yahk! Yahktivism had worked. I was more than excited. *The Hour* was going to Yahk! Everything was in place.

Well, almost everything: I still had no idea how I'd transport the snowmobile to Yahk. Only half of the whole "work itself out" thing had, well, worked itself out.

I went for a drive in the Corolla to do some errands and try and sort things out. Mr Ed said hello. I flipped him open.

"Hello," I said.

"Hi, can I speak to Kyle?"

"Yep, speaking. Who's this?"

"My name is Bruno. I work for Cintas."

"Hmm, I was wondering when you guys would call!" I said.

"You were?" he said.

"Yeah, well, I've worn Ricky's Cintas shirt on TV and stuff."

"You wore it on TV?"

"Yeah, on CNN and everything."

"Really? I saw you on the cover of *Le Journal de Montreal* last month."

"Yeah, I was there too. I've sorta been wearing it everywhere. It's a bit of an inside joke between Ricky and me."

Bruno laughed. "Let me tell ya, I put in calls to Cintas locations across the country looking for a guy named Ricky who was going around trading things. Nobody had ever heard of a Ricky. It wasn't until I went on your website that I realized your name was Kyle, *not* Ricky, you didn't work for Cintas, and that you were here in Montreal." Bruno had a smile in his voice.

"Hey, sorry to send you on a wild goose chase!" I said.

"No problem. I think what you're doing is really neat. I'd like to meet up with you and talk about the project and maybe see if we can work together on this," he said.

"Sure, sounds great."

"Dinner tonight work for you?"

I walked to the restaurant. I was really nervous. I wasn't sure how to approach the situation. The Cintas shirt was a joke between Ricky and me. It had inadvertently become my official trading shirt and uniform and was now an aspect of my trades that I'd never really planned on from the beginning. I really didn't want one red paperclip to become a corporate front for Cintas, not because I was against that sort of thing but because I had no personal attachment to Cintas whatsoever. The shirt was just an inside joke. Cintas, a massive corporation, probably just saw me as a publicity freebie.

I met Bruno at the restaurant.

After we'd met, shook hands, and sat in our seats, I looked him right in the eye and confirmed something I'd heard on the phone: he had a smile in his eye. He was excited. He "got it". It wasn't just a publicity freebie for him. It was *fun*. He was excited to be part of the project. The distinction between corporate executive and dude with a trip to Yahk dissolved. It was about people. Working. Together.

Bruno leaned forward and said, "I was thinking of offering you a cube van for the trip to Yahk. Would it be something you'd be interested in?"

I smiled. Then laughed. It was perfect. I looked him in the eye, opened my mouth, but Bruno said it first:

"This is going to be a lot of fun."

In a completely unexpected way, it felt right to meet Bruno. The shirt had come full circle to instigate a trade. It was amazing, really.

I said, "But why do you want a trip to Yahk?"

"I could use some time off," he said.

I smiled and said, "Sounds good to me. It's a deal."

And we shook hands.

"They" are you.

Whether they're a successful corporate executive, the famous host of a national TV programme, or just the fans of the "other" team, "they" probably don't know where Yahk is either. We're all quite similar, really.

If everybody wins, nobody loses.

If you create a win-win or mutually beneficial exchange, then everyone wins. Think about trade and exchange for a minute. It's all just win-win situations. This for that, that for this, those for these. Our lives are built around the idea of an exchange of goods, services, and most of all, ideas. Sure, you can form arguments about potentially exploitive forms of exchange, but can you imagine a life without the exchange of ideas? If you can, I'm amazed you can read this. Language was once an idea. Somebody told me that once.

People want to see it happen.

It's sure a lot more fun to watch things happen than watch things *not* happen.

one cube van

awkward pause
by colin pearson
WHATS SO GREAT ABOUT YOU?
I REPRESENT AMBITION ENTHUSIASM AND VITALITY
HOLD ME
I HOLD ONLY PAPER MY FRIEND
www.colinpearson.com

Bruno almost crushed my hand. He had the strongest handshake I'd ever encountered. And I'd shaken Al Roker's hand before. It was like some sort of medieval torture or martial art. I imagined Bruno being the world's only purveyor of a special handshake-based martial art developed solely for negotiation purposes. Brunoshake. Bru-No-Sha-Ke. It sounded Japanese. Maybe Bruno was a ninja. A ninja in disguise. As a businessman. You never know. It made sense, actually. He was quite the accomplished businessman. General manager of Cintas operations in Québec. Everyone seemed familiar with him in the restaurant. Maybe he was a *samurai.* I looked at Bruno with a sense of respect, and calm. I wondered if I should bow or hand him my business card with both hands, but I remembered something: I didn't have a business card.

Bruno smiled and said, "What are you smiling about?"

"Nothing, I'm just excited about this," I said.

"Yeah, this is going to be fun."

We both smiled.

Despite his abusive handshake, Bruno was one of the happiest guys I'd ever met. Energy eked out of him. He was positive, just like the direction of the trades. Bruno was happy in a way that made everyone around him happy. His personality was infectious. A good infectious. He was the kind of guy you want to be around. He was real.

And how about his trade offer! A cube van! The cube van would be the perfect way to transport the snowmobile to Yahk. I didn't mention it to Bruno, but a very small part of me wished Ricky had worked at Ferrari. But then I realized something: snowmobiles don't fit in the back of Ferraris. Yet.

Bruno must've caught on to my Ferrari thoughts because he added a bonus to his offer: "Hey, I'll chip in free fuel with the cube van. How does free fuel from here to Yahk and back sound?"

Wow. Fuel. I said, "Sounds good. Very good actually. You do realize I have no idea where the *back* part of 'Yahk and back' will be, don't you?"

"That's okay, you probably won't want to take that van too far *back* anyhow," he said.

Montreal to Yahk was a three-thousand-mile drive. Yahk was on the far side of the country, and as we already know, Canada is a really *wide* country. A three-thousand-mile drive isn't the sort of drive to scoff at, especially in a cube van. But I was up for pretty much anything. I bit my lip and let Bruno in on how far I was willing to go, "Actually, I'll take the cube van *anywhere* for the right offer."

"*Anywhere*? You mean anywhere in Canada, right?" he said, with concern in his voice.

"No, I mean *anywhere*. That's an *italicized anywhere*. For the right offer, I will take the cube van *anywhere*," I said.

"Anywhere in North America?" he said, his concern deepening.

"No, *anywhere*," I said and leaned forward to emphasize again that the word was italicized.

Bruno looked concerned, "So if someone from a place really far from Yahk, like Florida, makes you an offer, you'll drive it down there?"

I nodded and said, "You bet. If the offer's good enough, I'll drive the cube van from Yahk to Florida to make the trade."

I leaned forward again, lowered my voice slightly, and said, "Bruno, I'm not sure if you realize this, but if somebody wants to air-freight the cube van to Fitzroy Crossing, Australia, or Bishkek, Kyrgyzstan, then that's where I'll go to make the trade. *Anywhere* is quite inclusive."

Bruno thought about it for a second and said, "Okay, I'll cover fuel from here to Yahk, and then back to anywhere in North America, but air freight's out of the question."

"Of course," I said.

If it came down to it, I was certain I'd find a way to get the cube van air-freighted.

If it came down to it.

Bruno considered his trip to Yahk and said, "Since it's a trip for two, I think I'll bring my buddy from work, Garry."

I smiled and said, "Yahk's gonna be the best."

"I'm just glad I don't have to drive that cube van all the way to Yahk. I get to fly there!"

"You mean the plane will fly to Yahk. You'll just sit in the seat," I said, deadpan.

"What's that?" Bruno said.

"Forget it. It was stupid enough the first time." I took a bite of my food.

Bruno said, "Hey, I was on your website today and noticed Ricky's shirt could use a cleaning ..."

He then said that since Cintas was a uniform company, he'd clean Ricky's shirt free of charge. I jumped at the chance. This sealed the deal in my mind. I'm a total sucker for free laundry. Not only had I traded the trip to Yahk for a cube van and secured transport for the snowmobile to Yahk, but now I could also put off doing laundry for another week. Or seven.

I announced the trade on the website. People were excited that I'd made a trade, but the term *cube van* didn't sit right with everyone. People "had me know" that *moving van*, *box van*, *box truck*, *boxed lorry*, or *big van with a box on the back* would be a more palatable, universally understandable term than *cube van*. But Bruno called it a cube van, so that's what it was. There was no turning back. Although, with that in mind, a small part of me wished that Bruno called the cube van something much more random, like a pony, a denim shirt, or Amanda.

I met up with Bruno at his office in Montreal and checked out the cube van. It was massive.

He handed me the keys. I turned the key in the ignition. The van started on the first crank.

I visited Justin, who'd stored the snowmobile for me, took him out for a thank you lunch, and then rode the snowmobile up a makeshift plywood ramp into the back of the cube van. Once again, I wasn't wearing my helmet, and once again, I managed not to drive the snowmobile through the front of the van. Mom would have been proud. And when I uploaded the video on the

Internet, she was! Bruno arranged for some really sweet decals on the front doors. A picture of the red paperclip with the words: "Kyle – Not Ricky". It was perfect.

Dad came to Montreal on a business/help-Kyle-drive-the-cube-van-to-Yahk trip. We hopped in the van and drove west. We ate sunflower seeds. We went to Detroit. Dad bought a sweater from an outlet mall in Milwaukee. It was *legendary*.

A few days later we arrived in Minneapolis and Pops flew home. His co-pilot spot was filled by Dan, my friend from Vancouver.

Dan was in Minneapolis for a visit-his-girlfriend-Andrea/help-Kyle-drive-the-cube-van-to Yahk trip. Dan and I went to Mount Rushmore. We saw where the buffaloes roam. We shot a video of us watching the buffaloes roam and posted it on the website. It was *majestic*.

We arrived at the Canadian border just east of Yahk and pulled up to the guard's booth. The border guard strolled up, looked at the licence plate on his closed-circuit video monitor, and said, "Québec plates, eh? Are you the guy who's trying to trade a red paperclip for a house?"

"Yep, that's me."

"So, you're the red paperclip guy, huh?"

I smiled and said, "Yeah, I guess I'm the red paperclip guy."

"We heard about you on the radio this morning. It was in the paper too. I thought you might come through here. You're headed to Yahk, right?"

"Yeah, the CBC's gonna be there and everything. Everybody in Yahk is really excited."

His face broke into a big grin. "I bet they are. Wow, it's such a neat idea. Really unique."

He continued to smile, but then a frown came across his face. His sense of duty returned. He still had to do his job. This was a formal border entry after all. "All right, gentlemen, citizenship?" he said.

"Both Canadian," I said.

"How many in the vehicle?"

"Two."

"Where are you coming from?"

I pointed at Dan and said, "He's coming from the beautiful twin cities of Minneapolis and St Paul. I'm coming from Montreal … via Wall Drug in Wall, South Dakota."

"Where are you headed?"

"Yahk."

"Okay. Got it. Sorry about that. Still gotta do my job. Hey, what a cool idea! A red paperclip for a house, huh? We're all pulling for you around here!"

"Thanks."

"Have fun in Yahk, eh."

"You betcha."

We rolled out. Dan and I looked at each other with massive grins. It was by far the most surreal border crossing of my life. Dan can probably say the same. But then again, I don't know for sure. I'm not Dan.

We arrived in the Yahk metropolitan region and met up with Jeff at the hotel. It was great to actually meet Jeff after he and I'd talked so much on the phone. I'd come to know him as an ideas guy. A fast thinker. A photographer. A traveller. A do-er. Like Bruno, I'm sure he saw the obvious fringe benefits his company might recover as a result of the trade, but he kept everything very real and very down to earth. And in person his handshake was nowhere near as insane as Bruno's, so that was nice.

Bruno and Garry arrived. Mom and Dad arrived. Mom cut my hair and we all slept like logs.

The morning sun blasted through the curtains. Everyone met up in the lobby and we piled into trucks that pulled trailers loaded with snowmobiles. We hopped on the snowmobiles and went for a big snowmobile ride with lots of people for the final leg of the trip to Yahk. It's a pretty cool feeling to be on the top of a mountain with two-dozen snowmobiles, clear blue skies, and snowcapped mountains as far as the eye can see.

An incredible way to get to Yahk. It was a sixty-mile snowmobile ride but felt longer than all of Wyoming. And maybe even Montana too. Bruno and Garry grinned from ear to ear. There wasn't enough snow to ride all the way to town, so the trucks that pulled the trailers met us just outside Yahk and we drove the rest of the way.

I was nervous as we pulled into Yahk. The events that made Yahk happen were "unreal", but now it was totally real. There were people and vehicles everywhere. Cars, trucks, vans, fire trucks, police cars, a hockey team's tour bus, and more CBC satellite TV trucks than you could shake a stick at. There was even one of those dressing room trailers. Tonight the nation was going to get its news from Yahk, and Yahk had the dressing room trailer to prove it.

I walked inside the community hall. It was a television studio. Cameras everywhere. Long-haired men in black T-shirts ran around the building carrying cables. On the hips of their black jeans they wore knives inside leather carrying cases attached to leather belts. Roadies. George Stroumboulopoulos had *roadies.*

In addition to Strombo's roadies, hundreds of people milled about.

Everywhere.

I was nervous. I'd publicly declared that Yahk was the only place in the whole world I didn't want to make a trade. Maybe I'd be run out of town by an angry mob with pitchforks and flaming torches. It was possible. Then I laughed. People wouldn't be mad at me. I wasn't the culprit. George Stroumboulopoulos was the culprit. Even if he did have roadies.

A hand grabbed my head from behind and gave me an unbelievable noogie. I reeled back, broke free and spun around. A man with a grin from ear to ear stood in front of me and extended his hand.

It was George Stroumboulopoulos.

I smiled and extended my hand. We shook hands.

George smiled and said, "Hey man, I'm in Yahk because of you!"

I looked at him and smiled. "I'm in Yahk because of *you*!"

We laughed, because it was funny.

A woman walked around the corner and extended her hand and said, "Hi Kyle, do you know who I am?"

"Penny A. P. Anderson. I recognize the voice!" I said.

"Welcome to Yahk!" she said.

"Thanks, glad to be here!"

"Looks like that little petition worked out quite well, doesn't it?"

"I couldn't have done it without you!" I said.

"Well, that's what being a Yahktivist is all about."

It was good to be in Yahk.

Dan and I walked outside. I'd cashed in a heap of airline points to fly Dom out from Montreal for the weekend. She stood beside a puddle. I walked up to her, beside the puddle, and gave her a hug. We started to laugh. This was crazy. She looked up at my head and said, "Nice hair."

"Thanks, my mom cut it yesterday."

She laughed and said, "Yeah, it *really* looks like it."

"Then I wore a helmet all day today on the snowmobile and got helmet head. And then George Stroumboulopoulos gave me a noogie."

"Right ..." She said and stared at me blankly.

I don't think she was convinced. Or knew what a "noogie" meant.

I thought it might be a good idea to publicly blame George for my hat head as well, but decided to hold back. He already had enough on his plate. I figured if I said that "my mom cut my hair", then people had no option but to compliment it. It would insult my mom's honour to criticize her haircut. It was another loophole!

Dom and I walked inside the community centre. Everyone was ready for the big broadcast. We made some pre-show small talk with George and the many happy faces of Yahk. A group of festively dressed guys, about seventeen years old, walked over to George and me, and asked George for his autograph. George obliged. Then they asked for mine. I obliged as well. Dan came over and stood beside us. I said to the guys, "Hey, have you guys met Dan yet?"

The guy nearest Dan said excitedly, "Are you *Dan*?! From the website? The buffalo guy?"

Dan gestured toward himself with his thumb, smiled, and said matter-of-factly, "That's me, I'm the buffalo guy."

"Wow, can I have your autograph?" the guy said.

Dan smiled. "You got a pen?"

He signed his name. After all, he was *the* Dan.

The guy thanked Dan and admired the autograph for a moment. Then he looked up at Dom and said, "Hey, are you Dom?"

Dom smiled and said, "Yeah, I'm *the* Dom."

"Can I have *your* autograph?" he said.

"Sure," she said.

The show started. Live, coast to coast. George stood in the middle of the community centre surrounded by hundreds of Yahktivists.

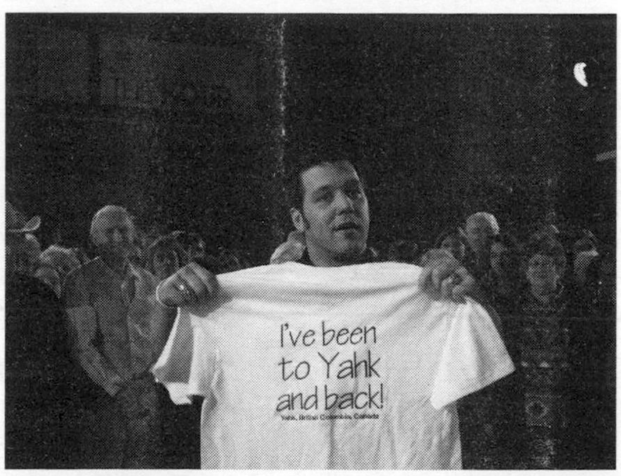

He welcomed the nation to Yahk and started his trademark rapid-fire freestyle news/discussion delivery of the day's current events.

Everyone was happy.

Hat head was now noogie head. Mom came over and fussed about. She reached down, picked up handful of snow, and tried to slap it on my head. I held my hand out and said, "I really don't think *snow* will help."

"It's worth a shot," she said.

I shrugged and let my hand drop. It *was* worth a shot. The snow was cold and refreshing like a piece of trendy expensively marketed mint gum. But thanks to George's knuckle prowess, my hair still looked like an eagle's nest.

I walked around and surveyed the scene. There was an entire hockey team from Creston, a nearby town, as well as most of the circa four hundred residents of Yahk. A van full of friendly folks had even come all the way from Seattle for the big event! They all wore white T-shirts with red paperclips on them. The "red paperclip guy" now had groupies.

Claire from *The Hour* said, "Five minutes to the first trade."

I nodded and said, "Cool, I'm just going to zip up to the bathroom real quick."

She shot me a startled look. "You're joking, right?"

I looked back at her and said, "Er, yes. I was just joking." I think I actually said *er*. But I know I wasn't joking. I had to go.

Five minutes later, George came out of the Yahk community centre, live TV camera in tow. I rolled up on the snowmobile to my "mark", pulled the key from the ignition, and stood beside George. We small-talked, then I introduced Jeff and Kerry from SnoRiders West. We quickly ran through the trade details. A snowmobile for the trip to Yahk. Jeff and Kerry had nice yellow signs to represent the trade. They handed me the nice yellow signs. I handed them the snowmobile's key. We shook hands.

I now had a trip to Yahk. Even though I was already in Yahk. And had already traded the trip away to Bruno. But I guess that's what television's all about. Lying. Ish.

Before we knew it, George said, "Well, we'll have to stick around and see what Kyle trades for next."

And they cut to a commercial break. The lights dimmed. I ran to the bathroom. Barely made it. I washed my hands and checked my hair. There were still bits of snow up there. I actually couldn't care less, but it was a bit of an insult to my mom's hair-cutting ability to let her down like that.

Live TV made me nervous. I'd stumbled a bit word-wise for the trade with Jeff and Kerry. I was lost for words, talking more nonsense than usual. Maybe I was just tired. I looked in the mirror. Large black semicircles were under each eye. I realized I hadn't slept well for the past week. All that driving. And all that not-sleeping. I splashed some water on my face. Excuses wouldn't help. The show must go on.

I walked outside, downed a cup of coffee, and ate a bowl of chilli. Claire came over and took me aside. "Okay, for the second trade, make it really exciting, *sexy* even. You want people to really feel your energy. This isn't just a trade, this is *awesome*."

"Okay, I'll try my best," I said.

"Great!" she said as she walked away. As she walked into the community centre, she nodded and gave me a thumbs-up.

I'd never had a trade coach before. Sexy? This was new territory. Wow. Sexy. Claire told me that this wasn't just a trade, this was awesome. And sexy. I thought about my hair. It just wasn't going to happen. Helmet hair always kills the sexy vibe. I reached into my pocket and pulled out a black toque. I admired it for a moment and slapped it on my head. It was perfect. A black toque was my ticket to sexyville.

With the stellar combination of Claire's coaching, my black toque, and my bellyful of chilli, the second trade was going to be a breeze. But not for Bruno. He was really nervous.

He took me aside and said, "What should I say?"

I wasn't sure, so I sent him in Claire's direction. She took *him* aside for a pep talk. With the cameras rolling, George came out of the community centre to show the nation the second trade. Bruno and Garry sat inside the cube van, just outside the community centre. I stood in front of the cube van and explained to George how Bruno had contacted me because of Ricky's Cintas shirt. George walked over to Bruno, who was behind the steering wheel, and asked, "Dude, let me tell you something right now. A trip to Yahk is wonderful, but *a cube van*? C'mon, are you sure you want to make this deal?"

Bruno, who was nervous and blinded by the light from the camera, stumbled and said, "W-w-w-w, it's done. I'm here," and smiled nervously.

George and I walked back to the front of the cube van, and

I said, "I will take this cube van anywhere in the world, *especially* Yahk."

A cheer went up from the crowd. It was all very sexy.

Everybody went inside. George and I ceremoniously cut a massive cake. The left half of the cake was a picture of a yak – a giant, long-haired cow-like animal – the right half said, "Welcome CBC *The Hour* No Trade in Yahk but Come on Back". It looked delicious.

George took a piece of cake and put it on his plate. In the distance I thought I heard somebody sarcastically say something about George having his cake and eating it too, but I can't be certain. I grabbed a piece and put it on my plate. I thought about placing it on George's plate, just for kicks, but stopped short. He already had enough on his plate.

Yahk resident and avid carpet bowler, Lee Rose, approached and extended his hand.

"Lee Rose," he said as we shook hands.

"Hi, Lee. I recognize you. Strombo had you on *The Hour* the other night by phone! They had your picture on the screen when you invited him to a game of carpet bowling on national TV!"

"Oh yes, well that was very nice to speak to George. And it was great that he carpet bowled with us. He's such a nice young man," Lee said.

I decided not to tell him about the noogie.

"Thank you for saying what you did about our town. It's the best thing that's happened here in a while!"

Apparently it was a good thing to go on national television and say you *don't* want to trade in somebody's town. I took note for future reference.

Lee invited Dan and me to come over to his house another day. The rest of the night was a complete blur. I met hundreds of people, posed for pictures, signed autographs, and ate more chilli.

The next few days, Dan and I went skiing with Mom, Dad, Dom, Bruno, Garry, Jeff and everyone else who could make it. It was great.

There's something inexplicably good about the Rockies in winter. I can't really describe in words how amazing the Rockies are, so I won't try. Let's just say if "nice" is the lowest thought-required complimentary adjective of all time, the Rockies are at the opposite end of the complimentary adjective spectrum. The highest-thought-required complimentary adjective of all time. Whatever that is. They're that good.

After our time on the slopes, everyone went their separate ways, and Dan and I hopped back in the cube van. On our way back to Vancouver, we passed through Yahk again to visit Lee Rose and his wife, Dorothy. They welcomed us to their home – a home filled with more than half a dozen Maltese dogs. Dorothy bred Maltese dogs as a hobby. Lee had written many stories. He read aloud several chapters from a book he'd written. A fictional sci-fi-ish book about time travel based around an actual rural homestead in northern British Columbia where Lee and Dorothy had once lived. I'm not usually partial to sci-fi, but hearing Lee's own words from his mouth was an incredible experience. There were portions of his story that literally sent shivers down my spine. He knew the characters and places so well it was as if they were real. And in our minds, they were.

We said goodbye to Lee, Dorothy, and their many Maltese dogs and started to drive out of Yahk. Just before we reached the end of Yahk, we stopped at the Goat Mountain Soap Factory. During *The Hour* broadcast, Mike Mitchell had handed me a bar of soap with a red paperclip in the middle and invited us to see his soap factory. I'd nodded politely, and said, "We'll try to make it if we get ..." but before I could finish, Mike raised his eyebrows and said, "We've got goats on the roof."

And that was all I needed to hear.

I'm just really into goats. White goats especially. I don't know why.

As you enter the small village in Québec Dom grew up in, St Alexis-des-Monts, there's a farm that has white goats. I always look to see if the goats are outside. If they are, it means good luck. But it's not a two-way street. If the goats aren't outside, it's not bad luck. It just means they're inside. Doing goat stuff.

The same superstition goes for black cats. My parents have owned a black cat nearly every single day I've been alive. Black cats have crossed my path countless times growing up, and I've had pretty good luck much of my life. So, I take it as a sign of good luck every time a black cat crosses my path. The same non-two-way-street rule applies: it's not bad luck if a black cat *doesn't* cross my path; it just means the black cat is elsewhere. Doing cat things.

Dan and I pulled up to Goat Mountain Soap Factory. The roof was goatless. Did Mike know about my soft spot for goats and had he lied just to hawk goat milk soap? It turned out there was currently too much snow on the roof for the goats. Mike looked up on the roof and said, "Yep, the goats don't like the snow."

I understood. If I were a goat I wouldn't like snow either. It being all snowy and such. Mike said that if we kissed Minnie, the "cutest" goat, we'd score free T-shirts.

Dan and I waved to Mike and Minnie from the cube van as we drove off down the Crowsnest Highway to Vancouver with "I Kissed the Goat" T-shirts proudly on our backs.

It was the perfect end to a perfect trip to Yahk.

I spent a day or two at my parents' place, hung out with Ricky, and generally "let it all soak in". A day into the soaking, I looked out into the driveway and saw the cube van. I'd reached a big milestone. Compared to a little red paperclip, a cube van is really, really big. It's amazing what can happen in only six months: from one red paperclip to a cube van. In Bigger and Better terms, I'd played the game well. If I put the van up on blocks, added a bit of insulation, and maybe a window or two, I could have lived in the cube van. It was as big as a house. I wondered if my parents would mind a big white cube van on blocks parked in the driveway. Probably not. But then again, I had no idea. I wasn't my parents.

Meanwhile, offers for the cube van poured in like crazy. This time I added my responses right on the website.

*******Hey Kyle,**

For your Cube Van I will offer you not one but two very well-trained cats. I have two black and white cats that come when you call them, sit, play fetch, high five, and shake a paw. I am

currently training them to do my taxes and cut the grass. I figure that with your publicity you could form a travelling cat circus and make tens of dollars. In addition, as I will not actually be able to part with my cats, I am offering myself as a personal trainer for you. I will follow you and your cat circus wherever you may go ... even to Yahk! Thanks for considering the offer.
Tom

Thanks Tom, This is a very considerable offer. Are you sure you're ready to do this?

*****I have a 1965ish 17" viola made by Hoff. It was once played by the first chair (and future concertmaster) of the Florida Philharmonic. He was my tutor for many years, but I stopped playing it some time ago, and it's time to get rid of it. It comes with a case, a bow, an extra string or two, and a shoulder rest. It's actually quite a nice instrument. Also, I have an original Darth Vader model from 1977 still in its original plastic that I'll throw in. While you're here in NY, I'll let you stay on my couch, and I'll buy you a beer or two. I have pictures of all of it, but not with me, so I'll have to get them to you later if you'd like to see them.
Neil

Cool Neil, I should be in NYC sometime soon. Keep in touch, I'll see if anybody out there wants a viola.

*****I'm willing to trade a 2001 yellow 11 horsepower thunder-cart go-cart, and my un-opened 007 40th anniversary Johnny Lightning die-cast model of the BMW Z3 that was from the James Bond movie *Goldeneye*. It's the size of like those little hot wheels cars and comes with a little mini copy of the original movie poster. It's officially licensed. I don't think it's as good a deal as that briefcase full of cheese ... Oh well ... Keep up the good ... um ... bartering!!

Yeah! Did you say THUNDERcart go-cart? Send a picture!

*****Dude
How about a two-week stay at my Florida condo?

Dude,
What part of Florida?

***** I trade you my skeleton playing a guitar incense holder.

Sounds really really cool. Does it rock?

*****I'll give you my autograph for the cube van I'll be famous some day this is the best friggin offer only 1 of my autographs exists in the world if you're interested email me.

Ah, somebody who understands the concept of supply and demand. Now, all you gotta do is get some demand and you'll be laughing all the way to the bank!

*****I'll trade you two trips to Yahk for your van.

Deal. Email me more details.

*****Dude, I'm willing to trade you 2 of my original paintings I did for my boyfriend, his singing Santa ... a Sherwood Place street

sign...and this 7 UP bottle sitting in front of me ... I'll even make you some ... CHEESECAKE ... haha ...
Jackie n Steven West Virginia (no we "ain't" hicks!) =) good luck

Cheesecake. Now that's something that'll twist my arm every time. Too bad you aren't hicks, hick cheesecake is my favourite!

And more than one hundred more.

After ten days of warm midwinter Vancouver rain, it had all thoroughly soaked in. Just as I began to get at-home-with-the-folks stir-crazy, an offer arrived in my inbox that really struck a chord. It was perfect.

"Hey, Dad, come check this out!" I said.

"What is it?" he called from the other room.

"I think this is the one."

"One what?"

"My next trade."

"Cool! What is it?"

"A piece of paper."

"What?"

"A piece of paper."

"Yeah, I heard you. I just don't understand."

"I think I'm going to drive to Toronto and trade the cube van for a piece of paper."

"A piece of paper? What do you mean?"

"Come here and I'll show you!"

"Are you just trying to get my interest up just so I'll wonder what it is?"

"Yes," I said.

"Like when an author writes something at the end of the chapter to entice you to turn the page and start the next chapter?"

"Yes," I said.

It was quiet for a moment.

"I hate when they do that," he said.

I heard footsteps. He walked through the door and said, "Alright, Dan Brown, you got me. What is it?"

You *don't* always get what you want.

Sometimes you have to put up with an *entire page* of nonsense before you can do what you really want in life. Like explore new places with good friends, achieve your dreams, or perhaps, most of all, read about pieces of paper in Toronto.

Luck is a four-letter word.

There's a popular idea that "lucky" people create their own luck by trying things and taking chances. You can't really argue with the fact that if you don't buy a lottery ticket you won't win the lottery. *Any* lottery.

Things are better now than they were before.

As soon as you believe there was someplace in the past where things were better than they are today, you won't operate at your full potential now. You are where you are, and if you aren't, it's probably a good idea to figure out how to get to yourself.

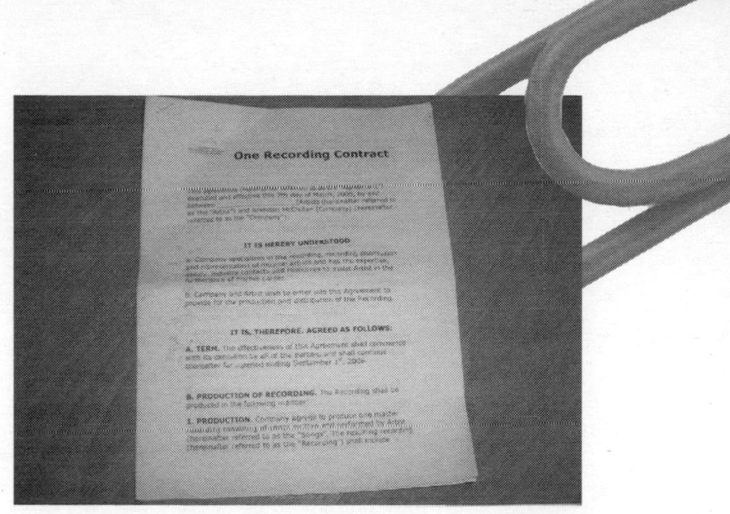

one recording contract

"A recording contract?" Dad said.

"Yep. Check this out," I said.

1. 30 hours' recording time at the #1 studio in Canada, enough for an album.
2. 50 hours' mixing/post production.
3. Return transportation to Toronto from anywhere in the world.
4. Accommodation in Toronto for duration of recording.
5. The album will be pitched to executives at Sony-BMG and XM radio.

I looked up at Dad. He smiled and said, "This is great. Somebody's going to really want this. It'll be easy to trade."

"And it fits on a single piece of a paper," I said.

Dad went back to not reading books by authors who pre-hype chapters in the other room and I called Brendan, the guy who'd offered to trade the recording contract. He picked up right away and we agreed to the trade. He was excited. So was I.

To make the trade, I had to drive the cube van another three thousand miles east to Toronto.

I went into the other room and said, "I just talked to Brendan. We agreed to the trade. Wanna drive to Toronto?"

"I've never driven east across the country," Dad said.

"Cool, you're in then?" I said, hope in my voice.

"When you going to leave, sometime next week?"

I looked up at him and said, "No, tomorrow."

"Oh."

The way he said "oh" wasn't reassuring. "Oh what?" I said.

"Well, I can't leave tomorrow," he said. "I've got stuff to do."

I thought about it for a second, but I couldn't possibly imagine anything better than a five-day cross-country drive in a noisy, slow cube van in the dead of winter.

"Well, I gotta get back to Montreal and see Dom," I said. "I've been away for almost a month."

"Hmmm," he said. "Thunder Bay. I can do half ..."

We booked his flight to Thunder Bay, where I would pick him up so he could join me on the trip. I called Brendan and told him I'd be there in about a week to make the trade.

I left Vancouver the next day. I drove north through Whistler and met up with Rhawnie, Corinna, and the red paperclip. It felt funny to see the original red paperclip after more than six months of trades. I looked down at it and said, "Wow, it's *the* red paperclip, but you know what, it's still just a paperclip."

"Yep, it sure is," said Corinna.

She looked up at me and said, "Hey, you're going to Toronto?"

"Yeah," I said.

"Do you want to deliver something to my brother for me?" she asked, hopefully.

I thought about the cube van out back in the snow. I looked at Corinna and said, "I don't know, it's not like I have hundreds of cubic feet of extra cargo room or anything ..."

"Yeah right!"

I laughed. There were actually many hundreds of extra cubic

feet of cargo room left in the truck. That's why it was *so* funny. Extra cubic feet of cargo room are like that. I smiled and said, "What can I deliver for you?"

She went to her room, returned with a box and opened it. Inside was a wooden fish. Corinna looked up at me and said, "It's a bit of an inside joke."

"I understand," I said.

"Yeah, right!" she said.

"No, for real. It's not like it'll be the first time I'll deliver a wooden fish across the country."

Corinna laughed. "Yeah right!" she said.

I gave Corinna a serious look, the look of a man with a purpose. "I actually have a bit of a history with wooden fish. I'm a bit of an expert when it comes to delivering them," I said.

"Yeah, right!" she said.

"A few years ago when I was on a ferry with my friend Mathieu in Indonesia I bought a wooden fish as a souvenir for a girl I was going to visit in Québec. A month or so later I arrived back in Vancouver, then drove across the country with my brother and a few friends. The wooden fish was on the dashboard of our van the whole way. We drove all the way to Québec and I delivered the wooden fish to this girl in her village. I was supposed to stay with her for a few days, but I haven't ever really left."

"Dom?" she said.

"Yes."

"That's awesome. So are you saying you might stay at my brother's place for a few days that could stretch on for the rest of time?" said Corinna.

"Stranger things have happened, but I don't think Dom would be too happy about that," I said.

"No, probably not," she said.

Two full driving days later I approached the Saskatchewan border. A huge green sign read "Saskatchewan, Naturally". Right beside the sign was a large green dumpster. It looked like an exclamation mark at the end of the word "Naturally." I thought how Saskatchewan is often the butt of jokes among urban Canadians because of its relatively remote location and relatively barren landscape. Either way, it seemed to me that the tourist board wasn't *relatively* helping the matter with their exclamation-mark dumpster.

I drove late into the night. I wanted to drive until the break of dawn, not because it made any sense but because it seemed like the manly thing to do. If popular music has taught me anything it's that there's nothing as cool as staying up all night until the break of dawn. Nothing.

The song "Running with the Night" by Lionel Ritchie came on the radio. I cranked it up and stared ahead into the black distance. The future revealed itself as the van rolled forward. I thought about the open road that lay ahead once I got to Toronto and made the trade with Brendan. There were so many uncertainties. So much was yet to come. I looked up at the stars and thought about how small the world is compared to the universe. I shot past a farmhouse and thought about how large the world is compared to each of our individual universes. I thought about how amazing it is that we can instantaneously communicate with somebody on the other side of the planet electronically, but how we often don't even know our neighbour.

A truck blasted past in the opposite direction, a wall of dry snow in its wake. I thought about how ideas can travel through the air, almost magically, but the transport of goods is limited to actual physical movement. I thought about how anyone who says the world is getting smaller obviously hasn't driven across Canada in the dead of winter in a cube van. I thought about how much better the song "Running with the Night" by Lionel Ritchie sounds when you're actually running with the night. And jacked on truck-stop coffee. Nothing's as powerful as truck-stop coffee. Nothing. The only thing that comes close is newsroom coffee.

After a fitful and frigid night spent in the back of the cube van parked beside a Wal Mart in -30°Celsius ice and fog-bound Winnipeg, I shook off the caffeine hangover, blasted the heat and drove the final eight hours to meet Dad in Thunder Bay.

We spent a few days with some friends, J.P. and Andy, whom Dom and I'd met in Portugal, then continued on toward Toronto. It was a great break from all that driving.

Along the north shore of Lake Superior we came across a frozen bay. People stood on the ice. Fishing. We pulled the van to the side of the road, walked down the embankment, and stepped onto the ice. We said our hellos and within moments they'd handed us fishing rods. I looked up into the sun. It felt great to stand, to be outdoors. If only on frozen water. Dad, ever the salesman, and a proud pop to boot, asked the fishers if they'd heard about the guy who started with a red paperclip and was trying to trade it for a house. I did that "Aw shucks, Pop" I'm-so-shy-I'll-kick-the-dirt move and nearly fell on my face because there was no dirt on the ice. That move works so much better with dirt on the ground. Sure enough the fishers and fisher women had heard about "the red paperclip guy". Dad pointed at me and said, "That's him!" I was shy. It felt kinda weird. I just wanted to have a friendly chat and stand on the ice. I guess he was just being a proud pop. Proud pops are like that.

We delivered the suitcase-encased wooden fish to Corinna's brother, Kyle. He wasn't really sure what to say. It probably wasn't every day complete strangers hand-delivered wooden fish to him. But maybe they did, I didn't know. We'd just met. He extended his hand and said, "Thanks?"

It felt nice to deliver the fish. I figured there probably wasn't much of a market for wooden fish delivery, but then again, I had no idea. Maybe everybody had wooden fish at home just waiting to be delivered to family members. After three thousand miles of heightened caffeine and Lionel Ritchie intake it seemed probable.

We arrived in Toronto and pulled up to the recording studio school to meet Brendan, who was in class. He came out to meet us and we said our hellos. I pointed to the van and said, "So you're gonna use it for your band?"

He looked at the cube van proudly and said, "Yeah, it's gonna be the ultimate band vehicle. We can put all our gear inside. Right now we use a Volkswagen Jetta to get to gigs. This'll be a bit of step up."

"It sure will," I said, as I stepped onto the oversize bumper to prove him right and to generally try to be funny with a *hilarious* visual metaphor.

Brendan coughed. Appropriately.

I stepped down from the bumper.

As a student at the recording school at the studio, Brendan got a cut rate on studio time. He gave us a quick tour of the studio. It was amazing. There were recording consoles worth more than a king's ransom. There were big black things with lots of buttons and slider bars and lights and small, expensive speakers and a glass wall that looked into a room with padded walls. It pretty much looked exactly how you'd expect a recording studio to look.

There were gold records on walls and autographed pictures of the artists who'd recorded there. David Bowie, Guns N' Roses, Tina Turner, Christina Aguilera. I thought to myself, maybe I'd get to trade the recording contract with Christina Aguilera. Or Axl Rose. I'm sure he could use some recording time.

We left the dark, music-making confines of the studio and went back outside. I turned to Brendan and said, "So, do you want to make the trade official?"

"Sure. What do you mean?" he said.

"I have an idea," I said. And I told him my idea.

I put the cube van in gear and shouted, "Ready?"

I glanced in the side-view mirror. Standing alongside the van, Brendan gave me a thumbs-up. My foot eased off the brake pedal and the van began to move forward. I looked in the side-view mirror. Brendan crouched next to the left rear tyre. He held the recording contract splayed out on the ground in the path of the approaching tyre. A gust of wind folded the paper over. Brendan reached forward with his hand to pull the paper back. The tyre approached. I put my foot on the brake pedal. Brendan's fingers were about to get crushed by a muddy tyre. At the last instant his hand came back across the front of the tyre just before it rolled over the paper. The left tyre signed the contract. It left a signature of mud and it missed Brendan's fingers by less than an inch. It's not that the tyre rolled fast, but it would've left more than a "mark" on his hand, so to speak. Definitely not the sort of thing he would've coughed about. I turned the cube van off, hopped out and handed Brendan the keys. He handed me the muddy piece of paper. We shook hands. It was official. He now had the keys to a massive piece of machinery capable of crossing continents. I had a piece of paper. And a promise.

We said our "see ya laters" and walked to our rental car. I can't recall the model, but I can assure you it wasn't a Dodge Stratus. I would've remembered *that*. So feel free to visualize any sort of mid-sized American sedan, *except* a Dodge Stratus. That'd be inaccurate. Dad shifted into D and we got on the highway toward Montreal.

I picked up the recording contract and held it in my hands. Sure it was just a piece of paper, but it was so much more. No longer was one red paperclip about ever-larger objects; it was about potential. The piece of paper in my hand wasn't just a piece of paper; it was an opportunity, an opportunity that could open the door for somebody, or even a group of people. But not me, someone else. My musical aptitude started and stopped at the keyboard bass line to "My Prerogative" by Bobby Brown. So, the recording contract was pretty useless to me unless Bobby Brown was waiting for a skinny white kid from Canada to rock the keys on a hot new remix. You never know, but I wasn't betting on it. But for somebody else, the funtential of this piece of paper was immense. Somebody could get signed by a label, go on tour, and have groupies and, even better, roadies. Imagine that, having *roadies*. I'd just driven across North America twice.

I was super tired. I'd gone flat out for over a month. Roadies would've been ideal.

I looked over at Dad. His hands were on the steering wheel. He stared into the distance. He was definitely keeping the show on the road. I guess Dad was a bit of a roadie. He smiled and turned up the radio and whistled along with the tune. I reconsidered his roadie status. He wasn't much of a roadie, after all: roadies *never* whistle.

We rolled up to our place in Montreal. One month on the road. Strombo and the crew at *The Hour* had upped the ante pretty hard with the trades in Yahk. After two drives across the country, and all those Yahktivities, I was a wee bit burnt out. No "woe is me" stuff; I didn't have it rough. I was just burnt out.

I realized my version of Bigger and Better had transformed itself from a pastime into a full-time job. Not a fourty-hour-per-week full-time job, but a twenty-four-hour-a-day, everyday job. Every waking moment and many sleeping moments, I was thinking about how to trade up to a house. My leisure time had quickly become work time. Who was I kidding? It wasn't a job, it was an absolute obsession.

Since my website design skills were horrendous, the vast majority of my time was spent maintaining the website and the "system" I'd created to help facilitate trade offers. The system consisted of my phone number and email address on the front page of the website, with the words "If you want to make a trade, give me a shout!" I'd stay up late into the night to answer emails, constantly improve the website, and try to find "the" trade. At this stage I figured it'd be fun to see if I could trade up to a *real* General Lee, the orange Dodge Charger from *The Dukes Of Hazzard*, with legendary flight and fishtailing abilities. I mentioned that I wanted to reach an intermediate trade item of a General Lee. At this stage, and in a stay-up-all-night-drinking-coffee-until-my-ideas-become-more-ridiculous-but-convincing-to-me state of mind, Dom would wake up, walk over to me, put her hand on my shoulder, and say, "You should really get some sleep, you know."

I knew.

But I couldn't pull myself away from the idea.

I wanted to make it happen.

I knew it was possible.

Even if I'd drunk too much coffee and couldn't sleep and was delirious and believed that fishing for a General Lee on a whim was the best way to trade from one red paperclip to a house.

Apart from times like this, I honestly believed I always put my best foot forward to make trades happen. But I was constantly nervous I'd get stuck and not trade up to the house. It's one thing to tell a few friends over beers that you're going to trade one red paperclip for a house, but it's completely another to tell literally millions of people all over the world that you're going to trade one red paperclip for a house.

Sober.

I didn't want to be the guy who *didn't* trade one red paperclip for a house.

It's probably not the sort of dilemma many people find themselves in, being the guy who hadn't traded a red paperclip for a house *yet*. I wasn't a politician. If I promised something, I would deliver. There was no other choice. I didn't want to look like an idiot. But I guess if I didn't pull it off I could always become a politician.

The offers rolled in:

Subject: I want it, I want it, I want it I want it, I want it, I want it I want it, I want it, I want it I want it, I want it, I want it I want it, I want it, I want it I want it, I want it, I want it I want it, I want it, I want it I want it, I want it

Kyle,

If you were to look real close at that contract you will find that it has my name all over it!! As far as music is concerned it is my life and I would slowly curl up and die without it. I'm sitting here in the freezing North East of England trying desperately to think of the one thing I can offer, and you will be able to trade. I have a General Lee!! it is unfortunately 6" long and made of plastic! I have two hard working children! But that's illegal!! I have a guitar and a voice, a dream and ambition, but you can't trade them!! The best suggestion that has been offered to me by a work associate is that I could provide my services as a naked house cleaner!! It works like this :- somewhere in the world there is a person with more money than sense who would like nothing more than to have a fit person to clean their house in the nude!! You may laugh and you may say," no way!" but believe me my good man, it takes all sorts!! I will offer my cleaning services for two months with no restriction on what type of cleaning is undertaken. I'll do guttering, gardening, dusting, vacuuming, you name it. As a bonus, when I make my millions with the contract I will buy you that General Lee!!! Do we have a deal? This is by far the most obscure e-mail I have ever produced, please do not let it be in vain!

Yours (with nothing more than a smile on my face) XXXX

The offer was sent from an email address that ended in @new.labour.org.uk. The Labour Party in the UK. XXXX was a politician! Or at least they knew politicians! I could only imagine the havoc this email could cause if I posted it on my site.

Public humiliation. Days away from work. It could be a media circus. It could flip XXXX's life upside down. It could ruin a career. Part of me wanted to post it on the site and see what transpired, the other half just wanted to see if, like me, XXXX was awake. I replied:

Re: I want it, I want it, I want it I want it, I want it, I want it I want it, I want it, I want it I want it, I want it, I want it I want it, I want it, I want it I want it, I want it, I want it I want it, I want it, I want it I want it, I want it
Dear XXXX,
I'm going to quote you on this – and make a tie-in to the fact that you're with the labour party.
Kyle

I clicked Send. Ten minutes later the phone rang. A frantic north-eastern-English voice on the line said exasperatedly, "Um ... hello, is that Kyle?"

"Yes," I said. "Who is this?"

"This is XXXX. You just sent me an email. Please, you can't let that email out. It could be quite harmful. I'm afraid I'll never hear the end of it. You can't tell others I work for the Labour Party. It could be the end of me."

"Don't worry. I just wanted to see if you were awake. I promise I won't publish your name or put your offer on my blog. You have my word," I said.

And that was that. I never heard from XXXX again. I guess XXXX didn't really want to trade for the recording contract after all. I made a personal note to stay out of politics.

Non-political offers rolled in:

*****Kyle,

It's me, CrittendenIV, from the Fellaheen Radio Network and the band MugWump. I once offered to trade you a musical experience on stage in exchange for the Yhak trip. Now, I have an even better trade for the recording contract. Kevin Hamlin, the guitarist for the band, is a professional tattoo artist in Corvallis, Oregon. He is my personal favourite tattoo artist. He is willing to trade an entire full body tattoo of whatever you or someone else wants tattooed across their ENTIRE body. This is a package worth between $20,000 and $35,000. Why is he offering this? Well, because we need to record the album in the proper way. :) here's a link to his work: http://fellaheenradionetwork.com/?p=570 So the trade for one recording contract could be a full body piece of art. Personally, I think the trade from a full body tattoo to a something else even bigger would be easy as pie. :) Let me know your thoughts. Thanks again Kyle. Have a great day man.

CrittendenIV

Hey CrittendenIV! My mom thinks this is the best thing ever. She's not into tattoos, but is pretty certain this is the best thing ever. I agree. This will be hard to top.

*****Kyle,

Here's my offer: one year free rent in the heart of downtown Phoenix, as well as roundtrip airfare for two from any major airport in North America. (If needed, the apartment could also come fully furnished.) Live right in the heart of downtown Phoenix. Short walk to Roosevelt Arts District, Major Arts and Entertainment Facilities, Sports Arenas, ASU Downtown Campus, the Capitol, etc. 1BR, 1Bath, historic bungalow style duplex with 9-foot ceilings, oak floors, living room with fireplace,

separate dining room, new kitchen, laundry room. 700 square feet. I can throw in four third-row tickets to an AZ Diamondbacks game, which is walking distance to the recipient's new home. I'll even fly up to you to make the exchange. :)
Jody Gnant

Wow Jody. A year is a long time to offer rent! I'm sure there is somebody in Phoenix or who wants to move to Phoenix who'll really like this. The baseball tickets might just be the icing on the cake.

*****Kyle,
My name is XXXX. I live in Los Angeles, and, like everyone else in this city, I am a singer/songwriter. I would love to get my hands on that recording contract. Here's my offer: my job. I am a copywriter for Lexus. I am offering you the once-in-a-lifetime opportunity to write exciting, provocative ads (that's TV, print, AND radio) for a luxury car company. Here are some of the perks: long hours, including nights and weekends; mind-numbing meetings; coffee that causes you to have conversations with God; free staples; copious amounts of rejection; window office that looks out on beautiful downtown El Segundo. Don't jump at this too quickly. Take your time. Think it over. Good luck with everything.
Josh

Wow Josh. You really know how to sell something! You should be in advertising! Well, I'm pretty sure there's a whole herd of people chomping at the bit to fill your shoes, so I'm adding this to the pile of offers.

*****Duke's Royal Spa Hair-Removal Experience

*****Kyle,

Ok let's get straight to the nitty gritty. I will trade for your record contract, one hair removal experience. I am in Tennessee and have a medical spa. I will provide hair removal for one man and one woman. Imagine a woman never having to shave her legs or armpits again. Or a man never again having to shave their face or no longer having back hair. With the magic of Laser Hair removal it can be a reality. It takes 4–8 treatments and costs between one and two thousand dollars per person. I realize this would only be useful to someone in TN or KY so maybe they could trade me something that you want. I want to make my second record.

Out, Duke Boles

Hey Duke,

You got that right: nitty gritty. I'm not the slightest bit interested in trading the recording contract for a two-person hair removal experience (which I'm sure is quite the experience), but I think you might've just dethroned the full body tattoo as the most strange offer yet. Props for offering something useful/funny. This will sure make it easier for on-air light-hearted small talk. Hey, you never know, maybe somebody will offer me something unbelievable for this ... Are you hairy? Do you live in Tennessee or Kentucky? Then make an offer for Duke's Royal Spa Hair Removal Experience

*****Kyle,

Hi there! I am in Nebraska and have an odd offer for this recording contract you have up for trade ... I work in a factory where we produce potato chips of many different varieties. I am willing to purchase and ship one case of chips or other snacks we offer every month (of your choice), for 2 years. Thank you

Jessica

Snacks for songs eh? I like it. Hopefully somebody out there likes the sound of a monthly snack shipment!

*****Hey Kyle,
I'm emilio, from mexico. I figure there are a lot of people out there who would trade their house for the chance to run a licensed bar right on the beach. A turnkey beach clubhouse with liquor licence with 2 rooms (one with ocean view!) to live in. With a little hard work you can earn enough cash in a year to buy a new house! So i'm offering to lend a beautiful 5000 sq feet club house in a lovely town 12 miles from acapulco bay. Only 3½ hours by car, 30 minutes by plane (the closest beach) from one of the largest cities in the world: mexico city its located right on the beach on the pacific ocean, on a favourite surfing and powerkite spot. we ran it for a couple of seasons as a kite centre but have recently renovated it to enter a small chain of restaurant-bars. all the necessary paperwork for it to operate is ready, the thing is we have done type of work (bar and entertainment) for a decade now and we're looking for new horizons so a break from the routine for some time would be nice. we are not musicians but have produced a number of pretty successful shows so now we're ready to try new stuff; producing a good record sounds interesting. The offer includes:

- 14 month continous "lending" (*comodato* in mexican legal rap) contract for the beach house, furnishings and food and drink equipment (fridge, freezer, stove, oven, keg machine, mugs, pitchers, plates, blenders, grills, neon signs, etc ...) we figure during the raining season its slow so we're giving out 12 full sunny months of work. During those months minor adaptations, planning and ajustments are ideal.
- the use for the duration of the contract of our well established commercial name: Burma Cafe

- Legal, supply (dealers) and commercial contacts and advice for the duration of the contract.
- 2 fully furnished bedrooms (TV, A/C, DVD, shower and WC) on the site for boarding for the duration of the contract
- 100 black and 100 red promotional freezbees with the name and logo of Burma Cafe
- 50 Corona promotional plastic mugs (more available through sponsorships)
- 60 Corona promotional keychains (also more available upon inquiry)

NOTE: utilities and operational costs not included. So go ahead! Live the dream of a bar on the beach!
Yours truly, Emilio

Wow. Now this is totally different than anything anybody has offered yet. Quite the opportunity! I think somebody will find this very very interesting.

*****Hi Kyle,
My name is Jacqueline. I was born and raised in Edmonton, Alberta. I heard you speak on 630 CHED the other day and found your story very intriguing. I left Edmonton in 1983 and moved to Vancouver with Dad. We started up a cookie business there. Needless to say I am still involved with it 23 years later. I have lived in Vancouver, Toronto and Phoenix from 1995–2004. Returned to Edmonton in April 2004. I started up a fundraising company called Dough to Dough. I sell to schools, soccer clubs, hockey, gymnastics, etc. Enough about me! Here is my offer: I have a diamond ring with 4¼ karat diamonds in it. It is 14 karat gold. I don't know what it is worth today but it was appraised at over $4,500.00 in 1989 (ish). So WHO KNOWS????????? I have a

friend who can appraise it within a day. If you don't like the first offer and you would rather have cookie dough, well, I have an unlimited supply and would be willing to bake some cookies for you to taste. YUM! Being from Vancouver I would think you would have heard of English Bay Batter. This is our family business. We make a MEAN cookie. Best you'll ever eat! Not sure how many cookies it takes to build a house but let's find out! Sincerely, Jacqueline – English Bay Batter/Dough to Dough

Cookies and Karats eh? I can't really think of anything better than IMMENSE amounts of English Bay Cookies. Growing up in Vancouver, I practically lived off English Bay Batter cookie dough (raw, out of the bucket). Hmmm, just thinking of what we can do to re-trade cookies or karats. If you have any ideas how we can set up something attractive to re-trade, let me know!

The offers were good, but something was missing. I got many calls from hard chargers, people who called up to make it very clear that they wanted to make a trade. Everyone made promises. I wasn't sure if every offer was legit. My guard was up quite high. If I sounded sceptical or unsure about making a trade with somebody, they often just pushed harder or upped their offer. Sure, I was trying to trade from a red paperclip to a house and I had to be somewhat shrewd and strategic with my trade choices, but it had to feel right. Sure, "the" offer had to be there, but it wasn't about the *offer*. It was about the person *behind* the offer. How could they use the recording contract. I wasn't comfortable to make a trade with somebody if it didn't feel right, no matter how good their offer was.

I couldn't decide.

I needed a sign.

The palomino came to life. I flipped it open and said, "Hello?"

"Hey, is this Kyle?" the voice on the line said.

"It sure is," I said.

"Hey, Kyle, this is Jody Gnant. I made you an offer for one year of rent in Phoenix."

"Hey! How's it going?"

"Good, you?"

"Great."

"Well I just wanted to make sure you had my offer. I think your project is cool and I'd love to be involved. I'm a singer/songwriter from Phoenix. The recording contract would mean a lot to me. I'd love to record an album of material I've been working on."

Something about Jody was different. She'd offered a year of free rent in her duplex in Phoenix. One whole year of rent. A substantial offer. But there was more to it than the offer. Jody was genuine. I was certain she'd use the recording time to follow her dream. To open doors.

I remained silent for a moment.

Jody said, "I think this will be an unbelievable opportunity for me. I've wanted to do this for a long time. So what do you say?"

I smiled and said, "Well, what do you want me to say?"

Talk is cheap and long-distance rates are dropping.
Today our talk can be distributed to the far reaches of the earth for less than it cost your parents to make a phone call to the next town. Talk goes farther, cheaper, and can be heard by more people than ever before. This means more people than ever before talk. But the same thing holds true for our *actions.* Our actions go farther, cheaper, and can be heard by more people than ever before. We have a choice, we can talk or we can act. We have a wonderful opportunity at our fingertips. Literally.

Some people don't like pickles. Others do.
In Junior High I took band instead of drama. I played the trumpet. But I didn't like to practise. I didn't have a passion to create music with the trumpet. The trumpet became a burden. I played the trumpet poorly. To me, the trumpet became a pickle. And I don't like pickles.

I knew full well I had no personal use for the recording contract I'd traded with Brendan. To me, it held no value. Like a pickle. But I knew there must be someone out there with a passion to create music. Someone with different tastes. Someone who liked pickles.

one year in Phoenix

So, that's what I said.

Jody and I arranged to make the trade in Phoenix the following week. She was very excited. She worked for an airline, and scored me a free flight to Phoenix. I wrote a blog entry about how I'd just traded the recording contract for one year of rent in Phoenix, then pushed Publish on my blog post.

And that's when things went haywire.

Websites everywhere announced the trade. It set off a cascading series of events across the Internet. When a popular blog or website posted a story of one red paperclip, a handful of others would do the same, and then another handful. It snowballed. Hundreds of thousands of people came to oneredpaperclip.com. Emails rolled in, and the phone rang like mad. I checked my email. Mixed in with the dozens of offers for the year of rent was an interview request from a reporter for the Associated Press. I made the call and told the entire story. Right after I hung up the phone it rang again. A producer from *Good Morning America* asked if I wanted to come down to New York and tell my story on ABC. The next morning a car was outside our apartment. That night I slept in a hotel room fifty floors above Times Square.

It happened that fast.

The day after that, on Easter Sunday, I woke up ultra early and rolled into ABC's Times Square studio. I downed a cup of newsroom coffee, *arguably* stronger than the stuff behind my hallucinogenic Lionel Ritchie experience somewhere in Saskatchewan, and was led to a chair across from Bill Weir in the *Good Morning America* studio. With Times Square as the backdrop, I told him the entire one red paperclip story thus far everything up to the words "wheat vine". Then we talked about my plan to keep going until I traded up to a house. Ricky's shirt was on my back. A camera sent the interview to several million people. Live.

It was all a bit surreal. I'd never said good morning to America before.

That night, ABC aired a segment about one red paperclip on *World News Tonight.* I was invited back to *Good Morning America* the next day to retell the story to the much larger weekday audience. I slept in the fiftieth-storey hotel room again. Monday morning I sat across from Diane Sawyer, Robin Roberts, Mike Barz and Charlie Gibson. The whole gang.

We talked about my plan to trade one red paperclip for a house.

It was all a bit surreal. I'd never said good morning to America before. On a Monday.

Then the Associated Press article about one red paperclip was released.

The very same day.

It was picked up by hundreds and hundreds of newspapers, websites, and TV shows all over the world. If I didn't know better, I'd say that this was the exact point in which one red paperclip "tipped", in the public eye at least. But I did know better. I had a cell phone. It rang incessantly. More accurately, this was the exact point at which one red paperclip "whinnied". In my ear, at least. People called up to say hi, how they'd seen me on *Good Morning America*, or to ask if many people had called up just to bother me. A few offers arrived as well, but I was totally incapable of anything more than the pen-notes-scribbled-on-hotel-notepad-shoved-into-pocket system. I was literally a fire hazard. I had kept my phone number on the website, so it would still be easy for people to send their trade offers. It was completely disruptive – but necessary, if I was going to trade up to a house. Something like forty thousand people an hour were arriving at the website. A *lot* of potential offers for the year of rent in Phoenix. In the midst of the mayhem, I ran down to the lobby and hopped in the ride service provided by *Good Morning America*. Between Times Square and LaGuardia I did five radio interviews. Three in the States, one in Australia, and one in Ireland. I hopped out of the ride, got on the plane to Montreal, and turned off my cell phone.

One hour later we touched down. I turned on my phone. The voice message box was full. The phone rang all the way through Customs. By the time I got back to our apartment, Canadian national news was on our doorstep.

We walked inside and I happily obliged their interview request. Anything to get the word out about the trade item up for grabs. The apartment line and my cell phone rang throughout the entire interview. Our apartment sounded like a horse stable.

Dom, Mathieu and Marie-Claude had answered the phone all day the best they could. With a frazzled look on her face, Dom dropped a stack of papers on the table. Phone messages. I pulled the wad of notepad from my pocket and added it to the pile. There were hundreds of people to call back. It happened that fast. Trade offers, interview requests, and just people who wanted to chat. With the pace the calls were coming in, it was impossible to return every call.

And the phone kept ringing.

The hype was in full effect. Tacky offers began to come in. Not tacky, but funny – like full-body-hair removal but tacky in principle. Real estate agents and online casino operators, who saw me as a fast track to quick publicity, had called. My phone was loaded with messages like, "Kyle, we're amazed with your red paperclip eBay trading. Please give our company a call. We've decided to give you a house. We just need you to wear our T-shirt on your website."

These people didn't get it. It wasn't about a red paperclip or a house, it was about people.

Working.

Together.

And I'd never used eBay to trade things.

I could always pick out somebody who was making a trade offer for all the wrong reasons. They would never say hello. It was always the product first. It felt fake. Not surreal, but fake. So fake. So exactly the opposite of everything I'd set out to do. I couldn't imagine throwing everything away for a "free" house. To help weed out the insincere offers, I asked everyone the same question:

"Why do you want a year of free rent in Phoenix?"

They'd often say, "Well, we don't want the year of free rent. We want to offer you a house."

"So what will you do with the free year of rent then?" I said.

"Actually, we've never really thought about that. We just think it will be good publicity for us."

Someone actually said that.

I said, "I appreciate the offer, but I want to trade with somebody who will use the year of rent."

And we went our separate ways.

I thought about how a person in high demand could easily slide into a lifestyle against his principles. It could all go sour so easily, and be gone forever. I had to be careful. The next time I might not meet friendly firefighters with Tootsie Pops and Dalmatians.

I didn't really sleep that night. Between 6:00 a.m. and noon the next day I'd done at least thirty phone interviews and was running late for the flight to Phoenix. I had to pack and hail a cab fast, or miss the flight. By now, articles about one red paperclip from the Associated Press wire had appeared in hundreds of newspapers around the planet. The phone rang continuously, like water pouring from a tap. Horse-flavoured water. After a brief overnight hiatus, the stable was back in operation. I stuffed some clothes in my backpack and answered a call. It was a woman named Stephanie. She said, "My daughter Jaclyn and I live in Montreal and we've followed your trading adventure for months. We're big fans of the project and wonder if you'd like to trade one of your red paperclip patches for some Girl Scout cookies?"

On any other day this would've been the best offer ever. Girl Scout cookies are the best. But I was late for my flight and had to hustle and find a cab. Stat.

"I'd love to make a trade, but I'm just about to leave downtown Montreal for the airport," I said.

"Really? We live near the airport. We're downtown right now, and on our way home. Do you need a lift?"

"That'd be great!" I said.

Stephanie and Jaclyn swung by my apartment, we made the trade, and they dropped me off at the airport. All taxis should provide Girl Scout cookies. And be driven by cheerful women and their daughters. And have telepathy.

I had a two-hour stopover in Philadelphia. I walked off the plane, cracked open the box of cookies, stuffed one in my mouth and turned my phone on. It whinnied immediately. I flipped it open and said, "Hewwo?" through a mouthful of cookie.

"Helloy, is this Koyle?" said a very chipper Australian man.

"Yehp, tha's mwe," I said quietly as I found a quiet corner near the gate next to a bank of payphones and swallowed the rest of the cookie.

"Good morning mate! I'm calling from a radio station in Melbourne, Australia. How ya goin'?"

I looked at the digital time on the payphone – 3:47 p.m.

I cleared my throat and said, "I'm *going* great, and a good morning to you!"

"Listen mate, we've heard about your red paperclip projict. Got a sec to chat on our breaky show?"

"Sure, but I'm due to get on a flight in about an hour. When do you want to do it?"

My cell phone beeped. It was another call.

"In aboyt foyve minutes, mate. That sound good?" he said.

"Sure! But can you call me back on another number?" I said.

"What's the numba, mate?"

My cell beeped again. I looked up at a payphone.

"Call me back on ..." and I gave him the payphone number.

"Country code one, right mate?"

My cell beeped.

"Yep, country code one."

"Righty-o, mate, so it's one-two-one-five, nine-three-seven ..."

"Yep, perfect," I said, cutting him off.

"Righty-o then, talk to you soon ma–"

I pushed Swap and said, "Hello?"

"Hi, is that Kyle?" said a college-age-sounding girl. "The red paperclip guy?"

"Sure."

"Wow, my name is Jenn! I can't believe I'm talking to you!"

My cell phone beeped. "Well, it's true."

And it was. I was talking to Jenn. Just like that.

"So, you put your phone number on your website. Do a lot of people call you and ask stupid questions?"

I coughed and said, "Sometimes, but most people don't bother, really."

My cell phone beeped again.

"So you traded up to a place in Phoenix or something? This is crazy, I can't believe I'm on the phone to you!" she said.

"Yeah. Listen, I'm not trying to cut you off, but I've got another call on the other line..."

"Oh, sorry about that. Have a good one!"

"You too," I said, and swapped the line. "Hello?"

"Hey, Kyle, this is Graham Hatch from Deam and Hatch on Rock 101 in Vancouver."

"Hey, I know you guys! I grew up in Vancouver!"

"Nice! We'd love to talk to you about your red paperclip thing, got any time right now?"

"Sure, but I'm doing an interview with a radio show in Australia in four minutes."

There was a slight pause.

"We can be done in three," Graham said.

"Perfect, but can you call me back on my other line? My cell doesn't have the best reception here."

"Sure, where are you right now? Montreal?"

"Philadelphia airport."

"You have another line at the Philadelphia airport?"

"Payphone," I said.

"Will it work?"

"Yes. I think."

"Okay, what's the number?"

I looked up at another payphone and gave him its number.

"Got it. We'll call you right back."

"Cool."

Payphone number two rang immediately.

"Hi, guys," I said.

"You ready to roll?" Dean and Hatch said.

"Yep."

Graham Hatch went into radio voice and said, "So we're here with Kyle MacDonald the red paperclip guy and ..."

Halfway through, a text message came in from a radio station in Phoenix.

Uncharacteristically, I multitasked a reply and asked them to call me on my other line: payphone number three.

After the Rock 101 interview was over, Dean and Hatch stayed on the line and said, "Thanks a lot, Kyle. Really appreciate it."

Payphone number one rang.

"No problem guys."

"Hey, will you be in Vancouver anytime soon?"

Payphone number one rang again.

"Um, maybe in a month or so. Not really sure."

"Well, if you are, be sure to let us know!"

Payphone number one rang again.

"Will do!" I said.

"Have a good one," they said.

I hung up payphone number two and picked up good old number one, my original freestyle office line. "Hello?"

"Good morning mate! You're on air in Melbourne, Australia. How you going mate?"

"I'm doing great! It's a lovely morning!"

My horse began to whinny.

"Where are you, mate, in a barn?"

"Nah, just the ringtone on my cell, I mean, *mobile* phone. Hang on a sec." I rejected the call. The mobile horse was silenced.

"Sorry about that. I'm good to go now," I said.

"Righty-o mate! So let's talk about your red paperclip adventure then!"

As the DJs gave their audience a rundown of the project, my phone whinnied again. Then payphone number three rang. I looked out the window. An airplane shot down the runway. The wheels left the ground as it took to the air.

I looked out another window and saw the airport disappear into the distance.

I awoke suddenly and looked around. I was on an airplane. Window seat. My shoulder felt wet. I looked down. Drool. I'd passed out hard after I got on the plane. The sugar crash from half a box of chocolate Girl Scout cookies will do that to you. The fact that I hadn't really slept in a week hadn't helped either. I'd done a handful of interviews during the two-hour stopover. A big handful. But missed a much bigger handful. There's only so many payphones a guy can commandeer. Dad had called midway through the onslaught. He must've heard the panic in my voice, because he insisted on leaving early for a business trip to Southern California to swing through Phoenix and help out the best he could. I gladly accepted his offer.

The plane touched down in Phoenix. It was midnight. A driver met me at the airport with a piece of paper with my name on it. Just like in the movies. He took me to a building, but before I walked inside I did another two phone interviews. Both in Japan. I walked into the building and did a satellite TV interview for *Good Morning TV* in the UK. After the interview, the ultra-chipper morning crew said, "Have a brilliant day!"

I looked at the clock. 1:30 a.m.

The sun is always rising somewhere.

I promised to have nothing short of the most brilliant day possible in the most chipper voice I could summon, pulled off the microphone, and exhaled. I was exhausted.

Jody and her boyfriend, Scott, arrived at the studio. Scott took one look at me and said, "Big day?"

"Yes," I said.

We hopped in their Jeep Cherokee and went to their house. I felt like I'd known Jody and Scott for years. It just felt right to be there.

We all agreed we should get some sleep. Jody had arranged appearances on a few local TV stations and we had to pry ourselves out of bed in just over an hour. But it was much more fun to stay awake and talk about stuff. That's the thing about stuff, it's just so much better than sleep.

"I'm so excited about this," Jody said.

"Me too," I said.

We smiled like fools.

Jody and Scott had plans. Jody worked part-time for an

airline but wanted to concentrate on her music career. Scott made furniture part-time, but wanted to quit his job to take the plunge with a custom furniture business. They had plans and were making moves to realize them.

"So what type of music do you do again?" I asked Jody.

"I call it Bohemian Geek Soul, or BoGeSo for short."

I laughed. Jody did too. I didn't understand at all what it meant, but it was a great name.

We did a pair of heavily caffeinated TV interviews on a pair of Phoenix breakfast programmes. I announced the availability of one year of rent for the right offer and Jody invited people to join us that evening for an impromptu party she'd helped arrange at Alice Cooper'stown, a restaurant owned by Alice Cooper. Since we were in the West, we figured high noon was the appropriate time to make the trade. Just before high noon, we went to the duplex to do so. Jody gave me a tour of the place. It was really cool. There was artwork on the walls made from recycled computer equipment.

"My mom made those," Jody said. "She finds things that are no longer being used and makes art out of it. She likes to make something from nothing."

I pointed at a piece that was made up of wide, flat-back computer cables organized in a pattern and said, "This one is great."

Jody smiled, and said, "That one's called *Byte Me*." Jody laughed. I did too.

We went outside and stood on the front porch. I squinted and looked at the sky. The sun was very high. High noon. I handed Jody the mud-stained recording contract. She handed me the keys to the duplex. We shook hands. Jody's brothers, Sean and Chad, took our picture. It was official.

I sat on the front steps and faced the sun. The sheen from my pale white arms and legs was enough to make a blind man squint. The sun was so warm. I now understood why so many people moved to Arizona. Who doesn't like the sun? I looked over at Jody, Scott, Sean and Chad. They stood below a tree. In the shade.

Scott smiled at me and said, "You can always spot the out-of-towner. The only one out in the sun."

I laughed, lay down on the warm concrete and thought about my skin being burnt to a crisp from three hundred plus days of UV bombardment per year.

The cry of a stallion pierced the air. I cracked open the phone and looked at the number. It started with a 61. Somewhere in Australia. I pushed Accept and said, "How ya going!" and got into it. It was a radio DJ live to all of Australia. After a few questions the conversation shifted to Jody. The DJ asked, "What toype of music does Jody sing, mate?"

I was about to launch into a quick, likely confusing explanation of what I believed BoGeSo to be, but stopped short. I smiled at Jody and said, "Why don't you ask her yourself!" I covered the microphone, handed the phone to Jody and said, "You're live to all of Australia."

Her eyes bulged. She said hello. Fifteen seconds later she launched into an improvised version of a song called "Red Paperclip". It was incredible. I think it was her first international concert.

We drove back toward their place in Jody's Jeep Cherokee. It had no air conditioning and the windows didn't roll down. In Phoenix. I couldn't wait to get out and stand in the sun.

A short while later, Dad arrived at Jody's place. He took a look at his pale, dishevelled, sleep-deprived wreck of a son who showed early signs of an epic sunburn, reeled back slightly, and said, "Big day?"

"Big week," I said. "Thanks for coming down."

"No problem. Just glad to help out."

I slammed an energy drink with an at-the-time-remarkable-but-ultimately-easy-to-forget-name, and Pops and I went to another satellite TV interview. This one was with Tucker Carlson. Tucker is the kind of dude that folks call a pundit. He gets his ass handed to him on a nightly basis because he says stupid and offensive things on a nightly basis to remain "controversial" enough to get free publicity so he can keep working at his job, on a nightly basis. The fact that he still has a job is a testament to how hard he works at his job each and every night.

He'd recently made headlines north of the border when he said Canada "is like your retarded cousin you see at Thanksgiving and sort of pat him on the head". This is actually something I agree with, in part at least. Canadians like to eat turkey, so you'll likely see one at a Thanksgiving dinner. The only thing is, if I had a "retarded" cousin I don't think I'd pat him on the head. I'd probably speak to him just like everyone else. As an equal. But that's just me. I enjoy a life where I *don't* have to say stupid, offensive things in order to keep my name in the press to ensure my ratings are up so that I get to keep my job.

The week before, Tucker had retired his trademark bow tie, so I brought along a flashing bow tie for the interview, just to keep Tucker's "dream alive", as I proudly told Dad. I sat in the chair in front of the camera and listened to the show through an earpiece.

Coming up on THE SITUATION you have to be some kind of salesman to offer a red paper clip and get a new house in return. You are about to meet a man who's doing it. An incredible story of trading your way to the top when we come back. Stay tuned.
(COMMERCIAL BREAK)

During the break, I spoke with Tucker by way of the microphone clipped to my stomach and fancy transparent earphones. He welcomed me to the show and asked if I'd ever considered moving to the United States. I said, yes, but I enjoyed living close to my family. I think many Canadians consider a move south at one point in their lives, especially during the winter part of their lives. As a kid in Vancouver, I always looked at a map of North America and wondered why I couldn't drive two hours south to Seattle and legally get a job, but I could drive for *six days* east to Newfoundland, an island in the North Atlantic, and settle down like nobody's business. Geographically, it was a wee bit funny. But that's just me. I'm into looking at maps.

Through the earpiece, Tucker told me he was a big fan of Canadian comedians, such as John Candy, Martin Short and Mike Myers. I smiled and asked if he'd help me get a work visa. He laughed, told me I was funny, and quickly changed the subject. He said he looked forward to speaking with me. I said the same.

I was about to be visible to a nationwide audience. I took a deep breath and thought about my hair. Was it messy? Or maybe it was just patted down. Sort of.

Carlson: Welcome back. My next guest may go down as the most resourceful man in all recorded history. Kyle MacDonald set out last July with just a single red paperclip and the goal of parlaying it into a new home. He started by trading the paperclip for a pen, he has since made surprisingly good progress toward his goal, so how does this barter game work? We ask the man himself. Kyle MacDonald joins us tonight from Phoenix. Kyle, you look great by the way.

I wondered if he was referring to my bow tie, or my hair. Or maybe, like me, he was in a studio without a monitor and couldn't actually see the person he was talking to. One thing was certain, my bow tie was sweet.

MacDonald: Thanks a lot. Check this out.

I plugged in the bow tie. It began to flash. I now looked like a clown. I looked into that camera and said, "Carrying the torch for all of us Carlson."

Carlson: Outstanding! I can tell by your accent Kyle that you're Canadian. Let me just say, as I said to you a minute ago in the commercial break, you are more than welcome in our country. We welcome you with open arms, truly we need people like you.

MacDonald : I appreciate it.

Carlson : I mean it.

And I think he did. Tucker and I spoke for a few minutes. He was very enthusiastic and encouraging. A real one red paperclip fanatic. Over the next few minutes I told the whole story of how I'd made my way from one red paperclip to a year of free rent in Phoenix.

Carlson : So where's this going to end up? What do you want in the end, control of the United States? I mean what's your goal?

MacDonald : It's kind of a secret, so I won't let you in onto it. But it is, like a subliminal form of world domination. But I think what my first goal will be is to get from a paperclip to a house.

Carlson : But are you going to keep going after the house?

MacDonald : Well, like I said, it's a bit of a secret. I can't really, maybe if you call me later on, but like I said, world domination. But the house first.

Carlson : Boy I think you're capable of it. Kyle MacDonald, a Canadian in America. Are you enjoying America by the way?

MacDonald : I love it. Sunny and hot. No dogsleds anywhere.

Carlson : It's the American dream man. He goes from a paperclip to a house. Try that in Canada. Kyle, thanks for joining us.

MacDonald : Hey, no problem. Have a good one.

Carlson : Thanks.

I enjoyed the interview. It was like a tailgate party. But with a flashing bow tie. I just sat back, talked smack, and looked like an idiot. Unlike Tucker Carlson, of course. He's an important news anchor.

I took off the bow tie and Dad and I made our way over to Alice Cooper'stown. A bunch of people were there, along with many of Jody's friends and family. People had read the invite on my blog and seen Jody and me on TV that morning. It was neat to meet people who knew Jody, and to see how excited they were about her and her album. It was a potential dream-come-true moment for her in many ways. A big push in her career. A risk, but a smart risk because she was about to follow her dream. Dad and I shook a lot of hands. It was a blur. A fun blur. The blur continued as we went back to Jody's place. I tried to sleep. It was impossible. I was too tired. And too wired on energy drinks.

The next day Jody, Dad and I went to the airport together. Jody was on her way to Los Angeles for a songwriters convention; Dad and I for other business. After dinner in Los Angeles together, Jody went to her convention and Dad and I found a hotel. I had my first decent sleep in ten days.

The following evening Dad and I sat in our room on the eleventh floor of the Hollywood Hyatt. The legendary Hyatt on Sunset. The hotel where rock stars threw televisions out of windows and rode motorcycles down hallways. A rock star's paradise. I looked over at Dad. He sat on his bed, stretched his arms out and enjoyed a massive, and surely satisfying, yawn. It was the second nail in the coffin of his would-be roadie status. Unlike people who read books that describe people yawning, or contain the word yawn, roadies never succumb to the psychological impulse and yawn. Ever.

Yawn. Yawn. Yawn.

I'd answered dozens of phone calls from people who'd made offers over the last few days, but aware of my tendency to scribble illegible trade offers on scraps of paper, I asked everyone if they could please send their offers via email. I then began the slow task of going through several hundred emails to separate genuine offers from all those addressed to the ever-popular Sir/Madam. It was a massive undertaking.

Secretariat rang. I answered it.

"Hello?" I said.

"Hey, is this Kyle?" a woman said.

"Yep."

"It's Leslie. We met the other day in Phoenix."

I'd met hundreds of people over the last few days in a sleep-deprived and distracted blur. The name Leslie didn't ring a bell. But I was too embarrassed to say I had no idea who she was. Maybe if I stalled for a bit, I would remember.

"Hey, how's it going?" I said.

"Great, how are things with you?" she said.

"Busy, but really fun."

I ran through the Rolodex in my mind. Leslie. Leslie ... Nothing.

Leslie, if that was her real name, said, "Listen, I'd like to make an offer for the year of free rent in the duplex."

"You would, eh?" I said.

"Yup."

"So, what's your offer?"

"An afternoon with my boss."

"Your boss?"

"Yes, you can hang out with my boss for an afternoon."

I was in a tough situation. Leslie seemed nice, but an afternoon with her boss didn't exactly help with the whole trade-up-to-a-house thing. It wasn't exactly worth a year of free rent. I had to let her down gently.

"I'm not really sure how I can justify trading a year of rent for an afternoon with your boss," I said.

"You don't remember me do you?" she said.

"Um, I'll level with you: nope."

"I work at Alice Cooper'sTown. Jody's friend. I live in the

other half of her duplex. I had Alice Cooper make-up on the other night."

I flashed back. Leslie. Jody's friend. Worked at Alice Cooper'sTown. Alice Cooperesque eye shadow. Yes, I remembered. Leslie. Wait a sec. Worked at Alice Cooper'sTown?!

"Wait a second," I said, "Are you saying that your boss is ..."

There was a dramatic pause.

"My boss is Alice Cooper," said Leslie.

If you want to, you can.

Don't get me wrong. You and I probably aren't going to win the Olympic gold medal for the pole vault. Even if we want to. But it *is* possible. When I was fifteen years old I signed up for pole vault and tried it out. It was fun, but I never really got into spending hours to perfect the fine art of launching my body over a bar with a pole. Maybe if I'd had a stronger passion to launch myself over a bar with a pole I would've worked harder at it and someday vaulted myself over a bar with a pole higher than anyone had ever vaulted over a bar with a pole before. But, somebody out there wants to win the Olympic gold medal for pole vault. And will.

If you don't try, you'll never know.

If I'd never tried pole vault I would've spent an entire day in tenth grade *not* doing pole vault at the district championships. I think it's way better to launch yourself over a bar with a pole than *not* to launch yourself over a bar with a pole. If I'd never tried, I would never have known that I *could* launch myself over a bar with a pole. I might have spent the rest of my life deep in thought, wondering if I could launch myself over a bar with a pole. I might not be an Olympic gold medal-winning pole vaulter, but I can look anybody straight in the eye and say that I can launch myself over a bar with a pole. And believe me, when you know you're able to do something like that, it gives you incredible peace of mind. Even if you came in last place.

It's easier to be yourself when you're actually there.

If I were beside you right now I'd probably want to hear what you have to say. You can interact with email, phone, video, messaging, and all the rest, but that doesn't mean you are really *you*. It's still not a handshake. Besides, not everyone answers their phone. Or checks their phone messages. Or has a phone. Or wants one.

one afternoon with Alice Cooper

I accepted Leslie's offer right away. I'd never had the opportunity to spend an afternoon with a rock legend before. It didn't seem like the kind of opportunity that came along very often. Then I thought about it for a second. If I planned to trade up to a house, I'd have to retrade the afternoon with Alice Cooper with somebody else. I was sure the opportunity to *trade* an afternoon with a rock legend was something that *really* didn't come along very often.

"So does Alice know about this?" I asked.

"Well, not exactly, but I think he owes me a favour," said Leslie.

"But has he agreed to it yet?"

There was a dramatic pause.

"He will," she said.

"Wow," I said.

"So, it's a deal?" she asked me.

It was a sweet deal for Leslie. All she had to do was speak with her boss, and presto! One year free of rent. But she *did* have to move next door. I thought about it for a moment, smirked, and said, "Yes, but only if you move next door."

"What do you mean, move next door?"

With a smile in my voice, I said, "The free year of rent is for the duplex unit next door to you, not for yours. You have to move next door for it to be official."

Leslie said, "Um, yes..."

It sounded a lot like my "yes" when I "remembered" who she was. Well, whatever, at least it was a yes. I really wanted to see her move all of her stuff twenty feet, and since the other unit was a mirror image of her unit, everything would be in the exact opposite place. How funny would it be if instead of reaching for the wine glasses she grabbed a coffee mug instead by mistake? That would be the *best.* Nothing short of an absolute *laugh.*

"I'd shake your hand, to seal the deal, but I'm three hundred miles away. My flight back to Montreal has a stopover in Phoenix, so I'll swing by to make the trade official."

"Sounds good to me," she said.

I said bye and flipped my phone shut. Dad had left before Leslie's call, but he now came back into the room as I closed the phone and asked, "Who was that?"

"Remember when we were at Alice Cooper'stown in Phoenix and we met Jody's friend Leslie?"

He made a blank face and said, "Um, I can't recall."

"Well, anyhow, she just made me an offer for the year of rent," I said.

"Cool, what is it?" he asked.

"An afternoon with her boss."

"With her boss?" he said, and made a bewildered face.

"Yeah," I said.

"That seems a bit lousy, don't you think?"

"Guess who her boss is."

"Who?" He obviously wasn't in a guessing mood.

"Alice Cooper," I said.

He smiled, laughed and said, "Wow, really?"

"Yep."

"Are you going to make the trade?"

"Just did, on the phone. We should probably go and celebrate or something, eh?"

"Yeah, for sure."

I was so excited. I wanted to throw a TV out of the window and ride a motorcycle down the hallway to celebrate. I looked over at Dad, raised my eyebrows, and said, "Burgers?"

"Chicken," he said.

"That's what I'm talking about," I said.

It was the perfect situation for a high five. But I was too excited about chicken burgers for any of that nonsense. We walked downstairs to the closest burger joint and had a *huge* night on the town. Chicken burgers. My treat. I even ordered onion rings.

I woke the next morning with a smile on my face. This was an awesome move up. Totally unexpected. There was definitely a huge Alice Cooper fan who'd make an amazing offer. And best of all, this trade item wasn't limited to a specific geographical location. Alice Cooper could spend the afternoon *anywhere*. Leslie had mentioned that the potential trader could do a variety of things with Alice. They could go shopping together, jam together, maybe even go on his nationally syndicated radio show, or play golf. Alice Cooper had so much to offer. He was like a Swiss Army knife. A Swiss Army knife of awesomeness. The funtential was immeasurable.

Since Leslie was the prime mover in this trade, she got the free year of rent, and I got an afternoon with a rock legend. Alice really didn't get anything. Just the satisfaction that he'd made an exceptional employee very happy. I hated to admit it, but Alice Cooper was really just a pawn in the game. But a really cool pawn at that.

The next day I received a phone call from a television producer in Japan. He'd caught wind of my quest and asked if I was interested in coming to Tokyo for a few days to tell the whole story on a TV show called *Miracle Experience Unbelievable!* I said yes, based on the show's name alone, and a few days later Dom and I were sitting in a Tokyo TV studio. We were translated *and* subtitled and represented by actors who did re-enactments of all the trades. Then we walked out from backstage and surprised the audience, who thought we were back in Montreal. It was all completely unexpected – the trip to Japan for us, and the audience's surprise that we were actually there. I didn't understand a word anyone was saying. The set was yellow. *And* purple. It was awesome. *Miracle Experience Unbelievable!* The show more than lived up to its name. A surprise trip to Japan to create a full hour of prime-time television. It absolutely annihilated all predicted levels of good.

On the show, the presenter talked about a traditional Japanese fairy tale called *Warashibe Choja*, which translates into "Mr Lucky Straw". It was the story of a boy who started with a piece of straw, and after five trades ended up with a straw house.

I was in awe.

I had no idea what to say.

On our final day in Japan, Leslie emailed me. She had unbelievable news: Alice Cooper was on tour and had invited me to come meet him at his concert in Fargo, North Dakota! I was really, really excited, but also nervous. Wouldn't I use up my afternoon with Alice Cooper if I spent an afternoon with him? The experience promised to be amazing, but I was trying to trade up to a house. Alice Cooper is one of the more amazing and worthy guys out there, but no matter which way you look at it, he's not exactly a house. I was assured that my "afternoon" with

Alice Cooper in Fargo was just a "promotional" afternoon. I'd still have a *real* afternoon with Alice Cooper to trade.

Alice Cooper issued the following quote: "Kyle is out-Trumping Donald Trump. I can't believe he's getting me to trade myself for him to get a house, but it's just crazy enough that I couldn't resist. Whoever gets to spend a day with me better get ready for a wild ride!"

I rerouted my return flight to Montreal to make it possible. I still managed to keep my stopover in Phoenix, and met up with Leslie to shake hands and make things official. I then handed her the key to the other side of the duplex, and she handed me an Alice Cooper mask. I put the mask on and we shook hands. Jody snapped our picture.

I now had one afternoon with Alice Cooper and Leslie had one year of free rent. Jody and I talked about how great it'd be to crash through the dividing wall of the duplex with a giant axe and carry out a clandestine operation to move all of Leslie's belongings twenty feet to their new, and proper, home. While she was at work, of course. Jody said, with a sparkle in her voice, "Imagine getting *that* on video? The footage would be *incredible.*"

I turned to Leslie, "So, you *are* going to move next door right?"

She looked uneasy, and said, "Um, yeah … about that … Jody and I had a little chat. She thinks it'll be easier if I stay on my side and she rents out the other side."

I looked at Jody and said, "Is this true?!" in mock outrage.

Jody said, "Yeah, about that …" in a sarcastic apologetic voice.

I can't *honestly* say, true to the *purity* of the project and our *very official* handshake, that I was happy with the outcome. I felt that Leslie should move all of her belongings twenty feet and encounter unbelievable amounts of hassle, just to be true to the game. But it was settled. I just have to learn to accept the fact that Leslie would know where the coffee mugs were. She was going to stay on her side and get a free year of rent. Jody would rent out the other side. Reasonable? I *guess so.*

I stayed over at Jody and Scott's place. Jody had a few days off work and since she worked for an airline, she dipped into her free flight perks to zip up to Fargo.

We arrived at the hotel in Fargo and met Kristine, a producer on Alice's syndicated radio show, *Nights with Alice Cooper.*

We then went to the hotel lobby to meet up with Alice's road crew – Toby, Brian and Alice's daughter Calico. *They* were great, but I still wasn't sure about meeting Alice himself. I was nervous. After all, it's not every day you meet Alice Cooper. I'd listened to his music as a staple on rock radio ever since I could remember. I'd ever seen him "offstage" twice. Once on an Australian TV show called *Rove Live*, and when he did his "We're not worthy" cameo in *Wayne's World.* He'd seemed really cool on both of those occasions, but was it just an act? I wasn't sure if I was supposed to be afraid of the man. After all, he was *Alice Cooper.* I crossed my fingers and hoped he wouldn't have a snake around his neck today. Or dead chickens in his pockets.

And then he walked out. He looked exactly as you imagine. Black pants, black jacket, long black hair.

Alice Cooper.

No snakes today.

He walked over to us and said, "hi", and Jody and I shook his hand. Alice and I sat down and had some great getting-to-know-you small talk.

Alice Cooper and I.

In a hotel lobby.

In Fargo.

Just like old times.

Since Alice was about to receive the key to the city in the town of Alice, North Dakota, presumably, and hopefully, for no other reason than he had the same name as the town, we were all invited to come along for the ride. We hopped in a Ford Excursion stretch limo and watched the pancake-flat landscape of North Dakota roll past. The air was gray, the ground a mixture of brown and green. Occasionally, there were trees. And power lines. And cows.

As we neared the outskirts of Greater Alice, we pulled off the interstate. A car was waiting at the top of the overpass. Jody laughed and said, "That's probably a police escort."

Kristine said, "Yeah, right."

We all laughed.

We turned left and crossed the bridge toward Alice. The "police escort" began to roll. Then the lights came on. Blue and red. It *was* a police escort. That's what you get when you're a rock star, rural North Dakota or not.

There were signs on the side of the road that read "Alice, Welcome to Alice!" Alice smiled and marvelled at the scene. We then arrived in downtown Alice. Fans gathered in the center of town cheered the arrival of the limo. People were everywhere. Thousands. It was a mob scene. The limo pulled up and people peered in through the glass and shouted, "We love you, Alice!"

A handful of security guards pushed the crowd back and the limo pulled up to an opening in a plastic fence. A few minutes passed before the security guards gave the thumbs-up. Alice's managers and road crew emerged first. A cheer went up. Then the man himself emerged from the limo and waved at the crowd. A roar went through the air.

Alice was in Alice.

Alice made his way through the crowd and walked onto a stage erected in the town square directly across from a bar. He stood in front of the mic and said, "Has anyone been drinking today?"

The crowd went wild.

Alice spoke for a few minutes. He thanked the citizens of Alice, North Dakota, for the key to the city, told some jokes, and invited people to his concert the following night. It was an incredible moment. The thousands of fans of all ages who turned out for the occasion spoke volumes about Alice Cooper's popularity and influence over the years. To finish it all off, Alice pointed his finger at the crowd and said, "And when I come here, I expect to pay for nothing!"

A massive cheer rose up from the crowd. It was an impressive scene. Not bad for a town with a population of fifty-six.

As he walked back to the limousine, Alice signed autographs and posed for pictures. People knelt to the ground and said, "We're not worthy! We're not worthy!"

Alice rolled his eyes and smiled.

We hopped back in the limo and I asked him, "You get that often?"

"Well, not that much really. Only about ten times a day. Every day since 1992." He shrugged his shoulders and smiled, as if to say "What can you do?" Since it wasn't exactly the sort of thing he could stop, he might as well have fun with it. As the limo pulled away a guy chased it, knelt on the ground, and yelled, "We're not worthy, we're not worthy!"

Alice turned to us, smirked, then turned back to the man on the ground behind the tinted glass and said in an upbeat, sarcastic voice, "No, you're not."

On the ride back to Fargo the conversation shifted to golf. Alice Cooper is an amazing golfer. He has a four handicap. I'll level with you, I have no idea what that means. But whoever told me that fact raised their eyebrows when they said it, so I took it to be impressive. I mentioned to Alice that my grandpa, seventy-nine years old, had recently shot his age. Alice looked at me, nodded slightly with a frown of approval, and said, "Now *that's* impressive."

I'll level with you. I have no idea if it's impressive to "shoot your age", but Alice raised his eyebrows, so I was convinced.

We arrived back at the hotel, and the entire road crew and band walked over to a Chinese restaurant. Jody and I sat at the end of the table with Alice and his manager, Shep Gordon. The rest of the band and road crew sat at the same long table. I'd never seen so many roadies in a Chinese restaurant before. During his meal, Alice was approached by at least ten people who asked for autographs and pictures. He took it all in stride and had fun talking to everyone. I asked Alice if he was used to people approaching him all the time. He said, "Yeah, when it happens non-stop for forty years, you get used to it. But you know what? Today as we pulled into Alice with all the signs on the front lawns and the people everywhere I was intrigued by the situation just like anyone else. I've distanced my real life so far from my stage life that sometimes I forget that *I am* Alice Cooper. I have to almost shake myself awake, and go, Oh right, I'm *that* guy!" Just a regular guy like anyone else, but a regular guy whom everybody knows. I guess that's what happens when you're a living legend.

I found out that Alice hasn't had a drink in almost three decades, is a member of his son's school PTA, and drives a Smart car. He said, "Seventy miles a gallon. Seventy-five miles an hour. I love it."

I like the image of Alice Cooper, one of the most legendary "offensive" shock rockers of all time, behind the wheel of his ultra-compact car on the way from the golf course to a PTA meeting. In the general context and popular image of the man, that holds much more shock value than if he spent his free time biting the heads off live chickens. Besides, biting heads off live chickens is *so* passé.

Alice and I walked to the salad bar. As he tore apart a head of lettuce with a pair of tongs, an older fellow approached him and they started to chat. I walked back to the table to satisfy my craving for bacon bits. A minute later, Alice came back to the table and said, "Did you see that guy I was talking to?"

"Yeah," I said.

"Guess how old he was."

I washed the bacon bits down with a swig of water and said, "I don't know, seventy-five or so?"

Alice looked at me, a smile crept across his face, and he said, "Fifty-nine," and raised his eyebrows.

"Fifty-nine? Wow," I said, giving the raised eyebrows their proper due.

Alice's grin deepened. He said, "I'm fifty-eight. I feel pretty young right now."

He displayed a level of contentedness usually reserved for middle-aged women in the affirmation of looking young. But for Alice I think it went well beyond vanity or a feeling of youth. In the context of other rockers of his generation, it's a miracle that he's alive at all – something he likely realizes every day. He said, "The thing about me, when I was drinking I never got hangovers. I'd roll out of bed in the morning and crack open a beer to start my day. I was never sober long enough to get a hangover. And I didn't have hangovers for years."

His daughter Calico sat beside him. She heard that and shook her head silently. Her body language suggested that it was the first time she'd heard about Dad *not* having hangovers.

Alice said, through a mouthful of lettuce, "I just have an amazingly addictive personality."

I nodded silently. I really didn't have much to say. It was amazing to listen to someone be completely honest with himself. He didn't have excuses. It was all out in the open. Alice took a sip of his Diet Coke and said, "I think it's the wrong approach to try to stop an addiction. You can't change your personality. But what you can do is steer that addiction toward something better. The only thing I'm addicted to now is my family, performing, Diet Coke, and playing golf."

He spoke about the separation of his offstage life with his onstage persona, something he declared was necessary for the sake of survival.

"Offstage, I'm just Vince. If I tried to be Alice Cooper, the rock star, all the time, I'd be dead."

He went on to explain his thoughts about why so many famous rock stars had died over the years. As he bit into more lettuce, he said, "They tried to be rock stars all the time. And it killed them."

He'd seen firsthand how Jimi Hendrix, Keith Moon and Jim Morrison tried to live up to their onstage rock star image every moment of their lives, and how their bodies and minds were unable to keep up with the madness. Alice said he was writing a book called *Alice Cooper, Golf Monster* that would touch on those themes. He talked about how the stage persona of Alice Cooper, a vengeful madman, would view golf clubs as weapons. But the real-life, offstage Alice Cooper, Vince, viewed golf as a peaceful pastime, a passion and, in many ways, a salvation.

It was fascinating to listen to Alice in person. I couldn't wait to read his book.

We finished our food and broke open our fortune cookies. I forget what mine said, probably "You love Chinese food" – but I remember Alice's fortune. He put on his reading glasses, held the tiny piece of paper in front of him, and said, "No success is achieved without perspiration."

He looked up over his reading glasses, smiled, and raised his eyebrows.

I didn't need the raised eyebrows to tell me Alice Cooper was the personification of his fortune.

The fifteen-person-strong Alice Cooper crew plus hangers-on left the restaurant and walked into the street. A child rode by on a bike, waved, and said, "Hey Alice." Alice smiled and waved.

We walked across the street. A couple on foot passed and said, "Hi Alice!" Alice smiled and said hello.

As we neared the hotel, a massive mob of people emerged from a just-finished stand-up comedy act at the Fargo Arena. The crowd began to walk toward us, effectively creating a wall of humanity between us and the hotel. Alice's entourage sensed danger, and everyone circled Alice to keep him out of view to the massive crowd. A few people from the crowd expressed interest in the tight phalanx-type formation on the far side of the street, and I'm sure a few more put two and two together with the "Alice Cooper" marquee on the arena, the massive tour bus in front of the hotel, and the black-clad, long-haired entourage across the street. But we made it back to the hotel unscathed. If Alice had been spotted, I'm sure there would've been a chain-reaction-type frenzy. *Everyone* knew who he was. Something told me Alice would've loved to meet everyone, as he was a friendly guy and all, but at that moment he just wanted to go back to his room and watch *Jerry Springer* like anybody else.

We got to the hotel safely. The elevator arrived on the thirteenth floor. Jody, Kristine, Alice and I stepped out from the elevator. We said goodnight to Alice. He turned left and we turned right.

The next morning we sat in a radio studio with T-Bone, a DJ from Fargo's rock station. The studio was packed with reporters and cameras as Alice taped his nationally syndicated radio show, *Nights with Alice Cooper*. I was invited to join in as a special guest. For the "Closet Classic", I requested "Rainbow in the Dark" by Ronnie James Dio, which I thought was quite apropos. Without missing a beat, Alice related a bizarre gardening accident story in which Ronnie James Dio was attacked by a garden gnome. Apparently, when Ronnie was placing a heavy garden gnome on a steep slope near his California home, the gnome gave way and the two slid down the embankment together. His thumb was crushed between a large rock and the gnome. Dio ended up losing the end of this thumb.

My jaw was on the floor. It was, without a doubt, the best bizarre gardening accident story I'd heard that week.

Jody and Kristine joined Alice and me in the studio and we did a little radio theatre bit where Alice was burnt into submission by scalding-hot red paperclips. It was fun to record radio drama. Alice was like a cartoon character when he played "himself" in theatre form.

Alice and I discussed potential trading options. We came to the consensus that a European billionaire with a spare mansion would offer to trade me a house for an afternoon with Alice Cooper. But only if I threw in a red Speedo with the offer. With that in mind, Alice predicted it would be an Italian billionaire. He said something to the effect of, "Now Kyle, I know you're going to get something good for an afternoon with *me*, but can you just promise me one thing?"

"Sure, what's that?" I said.

"Whatever you do, don't trade me for a weekend with KISS, or something like that."

I said, "I won't do anything like that."

He nodded. We had an understanding.

We finished up the radio show and Alice and I walked around the radio station complex. We'd talked the talk, now we walked the walk. Alice smiled and said, "You know, a lot of people don't understand the stuff I do onstage or in my songs. They don't 'get it'. Frank Zappa once said to me about all this stuff, 'You either get it, or you don't.'"

I nodded. *You either get it or you don't.* I liked that.

We hopped in a truck and rolled over to the Fargo Welcome Center. On the way, Alice talked about the 1960s and 70s, when he hung out with older Hollywood stars, guys like Groucho Marx. He said that in the early days of his career people were scared away by his onstage antics. "We could clear out a room in five minutes, that's how freaky we were. But the older film stars 'got it', it reminded them of vaudeville."

I got the feeling Alice would've been successful whatever era he'd grown up in. He was an innovator, and naturally "on". He walked into the foyer of the Fargo Welcome Center, waved to the crowd, made a great off-the-cuff speech, and placed his hands in a slab of fresh cement. He was now part of the Fargo Walk of Fame. Forever.

We made our way back to the hotel. Alice went for a one-hour nap, a pre-show ritual and I took off in our rental car to the neighbourhood Wal-Mart in search of blank CDs so Jody, Kristine, and I could swap pictures of the weekend. T-Bone's rock station rocked from the car speakers. The afternoon DJs talked about Alice and me. They were into my trades and were excited about the Alice Cooper concert. The newscaster from the evening TV news came into the studio and said on air, "We were in the studio this morning with T-Bone and had a chance to catch up with both Alice Cooper and Kyle MacDonald. It'll be on Channel eleven news tonight at 6:09 p.m."

I thought to myself how amazingly accurate that was, almost *too* accurate. I was slightly spooked by the accuracy. Scared even. But then I saw a water tower. It was massive. A majestic beacon of top-heavy sky blue. The word *Fargo* was emblazoned on the side. I grew up near mountains so I'm always amazed by water towers. I can stare at them for minutes on end. They give me peace of mind. I admired it for a minute, then autonomously purchased blank CDs on credit from the self-serve checkout at the sprawling Wal-Mart adjacent, and made haste back to the hotel.

I flicked the TV to Channel 11 just in time and recorded the newscast of Alice and me. It was a great report. The newscaster even said, "Oh *Yah*" at the end, just like in the movie *Fargo*.

I rocked down to the arena and met up with Shep. We hung out near the sound boards and admired the warm-up act, Vindictus, a "viking metal" band. After they wrapped up, we visited Alice's dressing room and went over the plan for the end of the show. Alice sat in a chair, relaxed as could be, eyes fixated on a kung-fu movie. He looked up and said, "I only like the really, really bad ones. The worse the acting, the more I like them."

They give him peace of mind, apparently.

We formulated a plan and nodded to each other in agreement. Alice turned back to his kung-fu movie. Shep and I went into the arena to watch the show. A few minutes later Alice Cooper hit the stage with fury. He had absolute command of the stage. He swung a cane with authority and rocked everyone out. Hard. I was scared. No, really. I literally couldn't believe I'd recently enjoyed fortune cookies and low-budget kung fu with the same man. It was an absolute shock. A total transformation. He played all the hits, some new stuff, and had his head chopped off by a guillotine. His band, most of whom were at least twenty years his junior, loved every minute of it. They backed him up with an impenetrable wall of hard-driving rock.

As the concert began to draw to an end, Shep looked my way and we went backstage. The song "Under My Wheels" came to a close, and T-Bone hit the stage. He asked the crowd if they knew about "the guy who's been trading on the Internet with a red paperclip".

The audience cheered, somewhat. T-Bone wasn't content with the cheer and screamed into the mic, "We got a special treat for you tonight, *but you gotta make some noise, c'mon!*" and topped it off with the cupped-hand-fingers-being-drawn-toward-him gesture. The universal sign for "bring it".

The audience brought it.

I walked onstage, hoisted an eight-foot-long red paperclip horizontally over my head, and stood next to Alice. The band rocked hard as a mix of laughter/disbelief/cheers went through the crowd. Alice put his arms in the air to support the red paperclip and we both held it over our heads, and pumped it up and down with the beat.

I'm onstage with Alice Cooper.

On.

Stage.

With.

Alice.

Cooper.

I wanted to pinch myself to see if it was real, but both of my hands were holding the giant red paperclip in the air. I handed the monstrosity to Alice. He held it over his head for a few seconds, then brought it to his side, approached the mic and he said, "Oh thank you, Kyle, but you know I just couldn't take this without giving you something back."

I pulled my right hand out of my pocket and gestured, *"To me?"*

Alice said, "Yeah," and pointed behind my back. I turned around to see Calico with a giant red weather balloon over her head. I accepted the giant balloon and held it above my head. It was a great trade. A giant red paperclip for a giant red weather balloon. I looked out into the crowd of thousands and smiled with delight. A cymbal crashed and the beat increased. I was momentarily blinded by the spotlights and the intensity of the situation. Unknown to me, Alice drew a long dagger, and came up behind my back. He thrust the dagger into the weather balloon. It exploded. Since the balloon was filled with blood, the explosion covered the first few rows of the audience in blood. I was stunned by the blast and covered my head with my arms, now dripping with blood. I turned around only to be blasted by a stream of blood shot from a plastic container by Calico. I recoiled from the bloody onslaught and ran offstage in the opposite direction, completely covered in blood from head to toe.

The band brought it up to eleven.

The crowd went wild.

Alice hoisted the giant red paperclip over his head, grimaced, and heaved the monstrosity into the crowd. His rowdy fans promptly ripped it to shreds, as if it were a chicken.

That was the finale to the show.

A short while later I emerged from backstage, still covered in blood. A guy with a small piece of what was left of the giant red paperclip came forward with a black felt pen and asked, "Can I have an autograph?"

I smiled and said, "Sure."

I grabbed the chunk of former red paperclip, autographed it, and handed it back to its new owner. He thanked me, looked at me inquisitively with blood on his hands, and asked, "What kind of blood is this?"

A smile crept across my face, and I said, "Chicken blood, of course."

A week later, back in Montreal, I pored through the offers for the afternoon with Alice Cooper. So many offers had arrived that I couldn't add them all to the site or provide comments on my thoughts about each one. I wanted to try to get every offer up on the site in hopes of enticing a pre-offer from somebody else conditional on my acceptance of a standing offer. Like that last sentence, it was quite confusing:

*****Kyle,

I would like to offer you a trade for the afternoon with Alice Cooper. My dad is a huge rock fan (and a huge Bob & Tom fan ... that's how I heard about this trade). I would love to acquire this opportunity for him for Father's Day. In exchange for one afternoon with Alice Cooper, I am offering a gray 1988 Ford Thunderbird that runs great, although it does have a broken fuel gauge (I watch the mileage), a "disconnected" sway bar, and a hidden oil leak. In addition to the T-bird, I will include $200 worth of Tupperware (I am a Tupperware consultant), a batch of homemade sugar cookies, and a $50 donation to the Defenders of Wildlife in your name or a loved one's name. Please think about my offer because I would love to give this once in a lifetime opportunity to meet Alice Cooper to my dad.

Thanks, Rachel

*****WE HAVE A 1974 WELL PRESERVED FIRE TRUCK (PUMPER) THAT WE WOULD LIKE TO TRADE FOR THE ALICE COOPER DEAL. GREAT FOR LARGE-GROUP WET T-SHIRT CONTESTS & KEG RUNS. GREAT FOR THE HABITUAL DRUNK DRIVING OFFENDER, AS THE POLICE WILL NOT PULL OVER FIRE TRUCKS. THANKS FOR CONSIDERING OUR OFFER.

*****Hey Kyle,

i got a couple of offers for the Alice Cooper meet and greet, first of all i have a rolex watch authentic of course, 1980s stainless steel model in fine working form, i collect them so i only buy good pieces, or secondly i can offer a phone number which is quite famous its the JENNY song from tommy tutone, 514-867-XXXX ... anyhow i own the number and i get hoards of calls from everywhere from people wanting too talk 2 jenny, let me know, ciao and take care, Alex

*****Hi, I'd like to trade space for you for 1 week in my RV at Burningman. I have a 30 ft RV with air conditioning, shower, toilet, kitchen which will be well suited for spending the week in during the heat and playa dust stirred up by the wind. I have all the towels, medical kit, and accessories needed for camping. I'll do all the driving from SF area, make sure you can shower and even have a golf cart to cruise in for the deep playa trips. I work at the BMIR Radio station, so you would be able, if you like, to join me on my nightly 9-10pm Sexy Sunburn Erotic hour of music show. I'll be throwing in some booze and hauling off your trash for you. You just need to come with your clothes and your favourite food. Thanks for this opportunity,
Sunburn Sarah

*****I offer camping rights to our backyard for 6 months in Meridian Mississippi, one of the most boring and pitiful towns in the south. We are moving out tomorrow, and the house is for sale. We'd love to offer six months in our charming home's backyard, since it means folks from all over the world will see that it's for sale! By the way, it's a very reasonable asking price of only $99,000. On the event that the house sells before the camping (squatting) time is complete, the lucky camper will win an all expenses paid Greyhound Transport trip to the beach! Camping is such great fun, what else could you ask for?

And there were dozens more, but no word from an Italian billionaire. Nevertheless, I wanted to make a decision. Obviously the fire truck offer stood out from the rest with all those capital letters, but whoever sent it had done so by way of an anonymous comment on my blog, so I had no way to contact the offerer. And then there was camping in one of the most boring and pitiful towns in the South. How could I decide? But as was the case all along, it wasn't really about the offer, it was about the *offerer.*

I wanted to trade with an Alice Cooper fan. Someone who stepped up with a decent offer but made it easy for me to decide because they wanted to become involved.

The phone rang.

I answered it. It was Mark Herrmann from Kentucky. He'd made an offer by email for a guitar or something like that. I couldn't recall exactly. We talked for a while. He seemed like a really good guy. A classic rock fan who really wanted to meet Alice Cooper. He had guitars and drums and other memorabilia he could trade. It was hard to break it to him, but I wasn't prepared to trade things like that for an afternoon with Alice Cooper. I'd put so much time and effort into the trades thus far. I wanted to move up. Sure, the value of an afternoon with Alice Cooper was completely relative, depending on the degree of Alice Cooper fan a person was. People all over the world followed my progress on a daily basis. Everyone wanted, or even expected, someone wealthy to step up and offer a house. Perhaps that red Speedo-clad Italian billionaire. People followed my trading progress and were literally gunning for me to trade up to the house. I couldn't let them down. Mark understood. At a very awkward moment in the conversation, he explained how he was an aspiring concert photographer. A chance for him to meet and possibly take pictures with Alice Cooper might help him find his "in" in that career. This trade could make all the difference for him.

All the difference.

A flashbulb went off in my head. Something crazy came to my mind. Very crazy. Crazy enough to work.

I smiled and said, "Hey, you might think I'm a bit of a lunatic for what I'm about to say, but do you have any snow globes?"

"Like those things filled with water that you shake up so it looks like it's snowing?" he said.

"Yeah," I said.

"Sure, I got some snow globes," he said.

"Really?"

"Yeah, my mom's got a *Phantom of the Opera* snow globe. I've got a couple of others too."

"How many others do you have?"

"Oh, I dunno. Five, six maybe." He answered pretty fast, all things considered. It's not the sort of question you really ever get asked. *How many snow globes do you have?*

"Would you be willing to trade one of your snow globes for an afternoon with Alice Cooper?"

"Yes," he replied.

I leaned forward and said, "What's the best snow globe you have?"

"My best snow globe?" he said.

"Yeah, your best snow globe," I said.

He thought about it for a moment.

"Well, I'd have to say that my *best* snow globe is..."

What picture are you painting?

People always say things like "I'm not an artist. I can't draw." But most artists don't draw, they *paint pictures.* Often just in people's minds. Think about Alice Cooper. He's painted elaborate pictures in people's minds for more than four decades. And it's not just artists; *everyone* paints pictures. In business, there's the term "the art of the deal", something I associate with business-people jumping in the air for celebratory high fives above a recently signed contract on a boardroom table in front of a Dry Erase pie chart on an easel. Business is an art, and the way you approach it paints a picture in the minds of others, as much as if you are a street performer or a sculptor. We each have our own style, and a way to approach a situation. Aggressive, passive, shady, smart, tactical, creative – all these aspects will change the outcome of any given situation. Your approach and the picture you paint will influence how others approach you and affect what you do next. Sure, it's *arguably* more fun to set up elaborate stage shows with guillotines and ghouls and raging rock and roll, in front of thousands of screaming fans, than learn about perspective and shading in art class or to put on a suit to jump over hurdles with a briefcase in your hand. But, then again, it's all about *perspective.* And possibly shading.

Everything we take for granted was once an idea.

Think about it. Electricity. Computers. The wheel. Houses. Everything. Language. Words. Books. Distractive, somewhat-related-to-the-narrative add-on text sections to add "texture" to a book, which are occasionally filled with a subtly self-referencing run-on sentence designed to confuse some people but give others a cheap laugh. At one time, all just ideas. If you can imagine something, it can be real. What do you imagine? How will you make real?

one KISS snow globe

And it wasn't just a regular old KISS snowglobe. Oh no. It was an illuminated electric KISS snowglobe with a *variable speed* dial.

A variable speed dial.

I could hardly contain my excitement.

A week later I stood on Mark's doorstep in Villa Hills, Kentucky. I was with Dad, Evian and Blago (the mad scientist/engineer behind Table Shox). We'd worked a trade show in Chicago, made the three-hour drive south to Indianapolis, slept, woken up, and made the short two-hour drive to Mark's doorstep in Kentucky, just south of Cincinnati. Mark welcomed us inside. He seemed a bit nervous. He and I had spoken on the phone a few times over the last week or two, but my dad, Evian and Blago were never on all the extensions. I'm sure it's a bit more overwhelming to have four *real* people in your house than one *talk* person on a phone. But if he was nervous, Mark had his dog for protection. Bear.

Bear was the sort of small white dog you could easily punt off a drawbridge if it came down to it, but with a name like Bear, we kept our distance. I imagined how a bold sign on the front lawn that read "Premises Protected by Bear" would have been both humorous and effective, depending on the side of the joke you were in on.

Mark explained the name, "When we first got him we

thought he looked like one of those polar bears from the Coke ads on TV, so we called him Bear." It made sense.

I reached my hand out and carefully petted Bear on the head. He lost the attitude immediately, squinted and licked my finger. The name Bear was just a front. Bear was a *doll.*

Mark's house was like a museum of middle-aged suburbia. The scent of potpourri filled the air. The living room carpet was brushed in one direction. Small white porcelain Bear-esque doggies were scattered everywhere. One with its hind leg in the air, perpetually urinating on the leg of a coffee table. To each his own, I thought, but something felt funny. When I spoke with Mark on the phone I took him to be an upbeat dude. A go-getter. A hard rock fan – the last person I expected to unidirectionally brush his carpet or sprinkle potpourri in a wicker basket atop a pink toilet with a padded seat. I was concerned. I looked around and nervously said, "So, this your house, huh?"

Mark gave me a funny look and said, "Oh, this place? This is my parents' house. I'm just house-sitting for the folks. I live in an apartment. My place looks like a KISS museum."

I hoped it was true.

Mark wasn't wearing face paint but I wouldn't have put it past him. He *looked* like a KISS fan. Sideburns, hair done up in a stylish "do". He looked like a guy who listened to music. Definitely not a potpourri guy. But then again, you never know.

Mark was a former DJ and radio producer. He really wanted to get into concert photography for rock magazines. In a roundabout way, a trade for an afternoon with Alice Cooper could potentially help make that happen.

We took the KISS snowglobe out of its protective foam-filled box and plugged it in. Mark flicked the switch. It illuminated immediately. I turned the dial, and the electric motor began to whirl around the pieces of glitter. It was *super*. I pointed at the variable speed dial, and asked, "May I?"

Mark nodded.

I reached down and turned the dial. The motor began to whirl faster. The glitter swirled like a tornado. The light began to change colours.

The *variable speed dial* feature was more incredible than I'd ever imagined.

We couldn't peel our eyes from the snowglobe.

I turned to Blago and said, "What do you think?"

Eyes fixed on the illuminated and swirling glitter, Blago smiled and said, "I like it."

We carefully packed the KISS snowglobe in its protective box, and went out to the backyard. Mark and I stood on the grass and posed for the mandatory clichéd handshake picture.

As Dad pushed the big button on the top right of the camera, I turned to Mark and said, "I didn't realize Cincinnati was on the Kentucky border."

Mark said, "Yeah, I used to work at the Cincinnati airport, which is in Kentucky. People would get off the planes and say, 'I thought Cincinnati was in Ohio?' I'd always say, 'Oh, you didn't hear? They moved it.'

We all laughed. We had no idea they'd moved Cincinnati to Kentucky either. It was probably quite an undertaking.

We walked out front to our rental car to shoot a video for the website. Mark and I shook hands once again to make the trade official, but this time he smiled mischievously, looked straight into the camera, and said, "No more Mr Nice Guy."

It was a great trade. An afternoon with Alice Cooper for an electric illuminated KISS snowglobe with a variable speed dial. I knew I'd made the right decision.

We went back to our hotel room in Indianapolis to "prepare" for the Indy 500 the next day. I pulled out my laptop and wrote a blog post to announce the trade. My brother Scott arrived at the hotel. I told him about the trade with Mark. He shot me a confused look and said, "You did *what*?"

"I traded an afternoon with Alice Cooper for a KISS snowglobe."

"Like I said, you did *what*?"

I held the KISS snowglobe in the air, smiled, and said, "*This* KISS snowglobe. It does have a variable speed dial, you know."

He squinted and said, "I know you. You're up to something."

"I'll let you in on a little secret," I said.

And I told him my secret. I didn't cup my hand to his ear or anything, because we were alone. That sort of thing was unnecessary. But if you want to visualize my hand cupped to his ear to create a better picture in your mind, please do.

When I finished telling him, Scott smiled and said, "If I weren't here right now, I'd be thinking *what the heck is he doing*?"

I thought about it for a second and said, "Yeah, I guess that's kinda the point. I want to see what people think about all this trading up. It'll all work out in the end. Trust me."

"*I* trust you *now*. But people who don't know what you just told me won't trust you."

"I guess we'll have to see," I said.

He grabbed our dad's computer and read my blog post about the trade with Mark. He pointed to the comments below the post and said, "If you ever decide to write a book about this, it's going to be pretty easy. People are choked. They're pretty much writing the book for you."

I walked over to the computer and said, "Let me see."

I think a little piece of me just died inside. I've been following this for the past couple months, and have been checking the page regularly. I was very impressed with everything you've done up to this point. Are you trying to get a house, or trying to make somebody you are trading to ridiculously happy? Or is this some kind of April fools joke in May? I'm sure you already know this, but the KISS snow globe goes for under $50 on ebay.
Anonymous

This is the worst trade that i have ever heard of, bar none.
Jared

This is possibly the dumbest decision I have ever seen anyone make ... ever. Except for the people on Jerry Springer. They make stupid decisions all the time.
Anonymous

Wow, I hope you're kicking yourself right now. I hope you're kicking yourself nice and hard. I knew you shouldn't have traded that

one year in Phoenix (which was a huge entrance into the real estate territory) for something with such relative value like an afternoon with a celebrity. And now look what you got ... a freakin ice globe (???). I don't mean to throw a wrench into your eternal hope and optimism, but there's a collectible store 2 blocks away from my house that sells that globe for $40. I wouldn't trade it with a smiley doorknob if I had one! I can vaguely hear your red paperclip weeping from here. Just WOW. What a total letdown. a sad day for the red paperclip.
Anonymous

I really think that you made one of the dumbest mistakes anyone could ever make. You should've gone for the fire truck or the T.V./sound system, anything that is worth more than $50 on eBay. You really did disappoint everyone who has been following your progress.
Anonymous

You traded for the SNOWGLOBE?! ARRRGGGHHH!!! I could've come up with something better than a lousy KISS snowglobe! I could've got the afternoon with Alice ... I'm going into the nearest corner, to cry myself to sleep. WHAAAH!
zoogirl

WHAT?
Anonymous

I just lost all faith in you and your trading ability. I have a doll house that is worth more than the KISS snow globe. How stoned did you get with Alice?
Anonymous

As with many others, I think this was a mistake. Big step back. Alice Cooper was a risky move in the first place, but there was potential ... But now a snow globe???? A few still have faith in you, but I wasn't sure after the Alice Cooper deal ... and with this ... my faith in you has been sundered. Destroyed. Broken. Lost. But I feel for you ... I'll give you a full sheet of drywall for the snow globe. Maybe you can build your house, instead.
Anonymous

I looked at Scott and said, "Yeah, you're right. If I ever write a book about all these trades, comments like that will put me on easy street."

"There's tons more too. You want to read them?" he asked.

I pulled a chair over, kicked my feet up on the table, and said, "That's what easy street's all about, right?"

You are mad mate ... I mean, a year's free rent in Phoenix was good – you might have got a downmarket house somewhere for that. An afternoon with Alice Cooper – well, there could have been a HUGE fan somewhere but a snowglobe?? You were really onto something mate and you had the whole world behind you. You've blown it now.
Anonymous

And thus this project jumps the shark.
Anonymous

You're 15 minutes of fame are about up ... After such a weak trade, I know I won't be following your site any longer ... I was really pulling for you to get the house, but now I see you're just riding the wave for fame ... If you'd of gotten something that

interested me, I would have traded one of my houses to you!
Anonymous

Worst trade, ever.
Anonymous

The snow globe! What??? Ow, my brain is hurting trying to figure that trade out ... I have been dropping by every week or so since I heard you on a Radio interview. It will probably be a while before I drop back again knowing it is going to take quite sometime before you get back to the stage you were at with the trades. I am still wondering if you know something about this globe that the rest of us don't know yet. Maybe I will check back earlier than later just to see if we are all mistaken on your decision about this globe.
Mark

Dumbass.
Ryan

Why oh why didn't I make an offer, any offer????? Now I think you might have been interested in my trade! arghhhhhh!
Anonymous

But not every comment came from someone with lost hope. Some people saw the trade for the KISS snowglobe as a positive move.

While I too think that the trade to the snow globe was a downgrade, I appreciate the fact that you are helping other people try to realize their dreams along your journey. Like you said about

the person dying of thirst in the desert – ??what's worth more to them?? – a million dollars or a glass of water. You could have traded the afternoon with Alice to a mediocre fan who had something better to offer. But instead, chose an avid music fan with aspirations of becoming a rock-and-roll photographer, to which that afternoon will mean so much more. If it was easy or quick to trade paperclips for houses, everyone would be doing it. It's not about the destination, but the journey it took to get there. Good luck and keep up the good work!
Brittany

Hey Kyle!
It seems that a lot of people have a lot of negative things to say about your trade for a KISS snowglobe. Perhaps these are the same people who said pooh pooh when you first came up with the idea of one red paperclip for a house. I personally say BRAVO! All good ideas deserve great praise and you have one really good idea going here. Good luck and a great journey on your way to your dream house. I'll be supporting you all the way.
Sam in Cape Breton.

Kyle,
I think most of your "fans" here are missing the point of it all. This isn't about getting a house. This is about the journey to get a house. You are just taking us along for your ride. I have never been on a good trip that has gone directly from point A to point B. You gotta stop and smell the roses, see that giant ball of yarn or world's largest Easter Egg. There might be a house at the end, but if you can't enjoy the ride home, why bother leaving? Keep on keeping on.
Jay

Don't let the naysayers get you down!
Anonymous

It is totally incorrect to equate "how much it would bring on ebay" with true value, or even trade-ability. Sure, if we calculate the monetary equivalent of each of these deals, one side or the other lost money. Then why did they trade? You got it – money is not the only, or even the best, scale against which to judge things.
abu

I read every single comment. It was amazing to see what people thought. Over the entire Memorial Day weekend in Indianapolis, I ingested a steady diet of intense comments, watched fast cars turn left for five hundred miles, then flew back to Montreal.

When I got back, I responded to the comment that I had "jumped the shark", by way of a video post on my blog. I placed a picture of Greg Norman, aka "The Shark", in a bowl of water and jumped over the "shark-infested" waters. If people were going to say I jumped the shark, I might as well actually jump the shark. I also added a link to the episode of *Happy Days* where a leather-jacket-clad Fonz sails off a water ski jump over a shark: and the genesis for the term "jump the shark" – the exact moment of a TV show when the writers begin to think of elaborate ways to extend the storyline of the series ... as some people said I'd done with my quest to trade a red paperclip for a house.

Nevertheless, offers for the snowglobe began to roll in:

*******I kind of piggy backed off your idea. I traded 10 points in a cribbage game for a banana. Traded the banana for a screwdriver that I traded for a can of soup. That can of soup was traded for a light that attaches to a mixing console. I traded the light for a**

microphone, then traded that for a better mic. (An Audio Technica MB4K Midnight Blues Condensor mic) I would like to trade this mic for your snow globe.

*****I will offer you either:
An autographed Super Dave Osborne show ticket
Unused, near mint baseball tickets: 1st game at Exhibition Place (1977) and last game at Exhibition Place (1988)
Collection of specialty Coke cans (empty. approximately 30 from around the world – Japan, New Zealand, Spain – as well as Canadian hockey teams, Blue Jays 1994 World Series)
Or all of the above

*****I really used to enjoy my trips to Montreal to watch the Expos play their very special brand of baseball, and eat french fries with gravy and cheese on them while drinking LaBatt Blue. I feel bad that Les Expos are no longer around, so I am going to allow you to choose from 3 (three!) offers for your lovely snow globe.
#1 – An autographed photo of baseball hero, and Mr. Steroids himself, Jose Canseco. Jose was my favourite player as a kid, and I was psyched when he joined the Expos. I was much less psyched when he was cut from the team a few weeks later...
#2 – A very large box of baseball cards. There are many cards in here from the golden age of baseball card collecting, the late 80's and early 90's. I will be sure to include cards of many great Expos who got away, like Larry Walker, Marquis Grissom, and Delino Deshields.
#3 – A family pack of tickets to see the Richmond Braves. Since the Expos are no longer with us, and I live in Virginia anyway, I now root for another awesome team – the Richmond Braves. I

would like for you to have the opportunity to see my new hometown team. Much like the Expos, all of their good players end up with other teams (especially the Atlanta Braves, for some reason). The family pack includes 4 General Admission Tickets, 4 hot dogs, and 4 12oz sodas.
Jeff

*****Hi Kyle,
My name is Dave Leroux. I am a retired movie star. My offer isn't worth much financially but the publicity you'll get trading with me is priceless! I've acted in a number of blockbuster hits including MVP 2 (Most Verticle Primate 2), Slapshot 2, and Airbud 4: 7th Inning Fetch. I am offering you Original DVD copies of MVP 2 and Slapshot 2 for the KISS Snow Globe. I am a HUUUUUUGE KISS fan. I Hope you consider my offer. I'll even autograph the DVDs! I have included a picture proving that I am the biggest KISS fan EVER! I'm the one wearing the Singapore shirt!
Dave Leroux
P.S. I.m the cat. Meowwww

The offers were good, but not nearly up to snuff with a KISS snowglobe and all its magical variable speedabilty. I read through the comments on the blog and noticed the following:

Hi Kyle,
Im jules from MTL ... I was up late a couple of weeks ago and i saw a show on TV on GSN (Game Show Network) called "I've got a secret" and Corbin Bernsen was invited and his secret was that ... he's a huge snow globe collector!!!!! Just thought I would give you a heads-up on that one. Cheers and good luck on all your endeavours!
jules

With Jules from MTL's comment, I figured it was safe to add the following trade offer to the trade offers section of the blog:

*****Hey Kyle,

I heard about your project on KROQ last month. I didn't really have a use for a place in Phoenix or an afternoon with Alice Cooper, but when I found out you traded for that glitter globe I stopped in my tracks. I've been collecting snow globes quite a while now and this is the kind of thing I could totally use in my collection. Not only do I want the KISS snow globe, I need it! (For reference, and I say this knowing full well it makes me sound like a total schmo, I'm the actor who was on LA LAW and in the Major League movies – and yes, those will go on the tombstone, I'm sure – here lies Arnie Becker and Roger Dorn.) Well, I've been redirecting that potential by making movies lately with my company Public Media Works. We completed our first film last year called Carpool Guy. My company makes movies specifically for fanbases. So this movie was made for Soap Opera fans. My offer for the snow globe is a credited speaking role in one of our upcoming films, Donna on Demand. I'll throw in a round trip ticket from anywhere in the world to the shooting location and will provide room and board for the actor/actress for the duration of their stay – per our need to have them there and take care of meals etc. If whoever you trade with doesn't quite fit the bill for a character in the film, we will write a speaking role based on their character into the film. We will also compensate them according to the union agreements we have in place for that film. So there it is, a Role in a Movie (sometime during the next year) I hope this generates some activity for you, either upward toward the house or lateral move for position.

Corbin Bernsen, President Public Media Works

Then I wrote a blog post entitled "A Special Message from Kyle".

Man was that ever a rad video of Fonzie on **Happy Days** jumping the shark or what? The best part is how at the end he hits the shore and walks away from the stunt. Fonzie is so cool. If you didn't see the original "Jump the Shark" video that spawned the term, check it out here. [There was a link to video on the word *here*.] Switching gears now. A lot. If you look through the current offers for one KISS snow globe, and comments on the offers for the KISS snow globe, and think about it for a second, I'm pretty sure you'll be able to figure out who I'm going to trade with next. I actually received the next trade item as an offer about a month ago, but I simply didn't have anything this person could use at the time. Because of this, I never guaranteed I'd trade with him or her. (Yes – I'm trying to keep you guessing who it is ...) I never sought out a snow globe and actually never thought of the snow globe up-trade angle until I found out Mark Herrman had one when he called ten days ago. The fact that it was a KISS snow globe was just icing on the cake. The cake of ridiculousness. Until Mark called I literally had no idea who I was going to trade with for one afternoon with Alice Cooper. By doing this move, I also wanted to see what would happen if I made a trade "down" for something – to see how people would react. The response made it clear that not quite everybody understands that this project is about people, and not the saleable value of objects. Mark Herrmann was the ONLY person who called me up and said why an afternoon with Alice Cooper was important to him and how it could potentially change his life for the better. He explained how he was an aspiring concert photographer and that if he could hang out with Alice Cooper it'd be a bit of a break for him in the pursuit of his dream. He got lucky because he was in the right place at the right time with (surprisingly, in this case) the right trade item. But he didn't just sit there on the couch and wait for his luck to happen – he made the call. He got involved. Sure, there was a massive case of "right place, right time, right trade object" going on, but in order for that to happen, you have to put yourself in the right place with something and just hope it's the right time. I could get really deep and introspective and talk about how that's kinda a great metaphor for life itself, but I'll use this somehow appropriate anecdote that features Darryl Strawberry instead. When I was a kid I collected baseball cards and read *Beckett Monthly*. It's what we did. I'd always flip directly to the back and check the current value of my 1986 Darryl Strawberry Topps card to see what it was worth. But did I ever sell it? Nope. Did I ever trade it with somebody for a pen and fill out a potentially sweepstakes-winning entry form? Nope – I didn't even take a shot at the sweepstakes – and I love entering sweepstakes. I just chewed my stick of rock-hard gum and dreamed about what I could buy with the $5.00 the card was "worth". (MINT COND) – So it was only worth what I thought it was in my mind's eye. I've so totally lost that card since then, and still haven't won the sweepstakes. Any sweepstakes.

So that's my message with this project I guess: something is only ever worth whatever somebody is willing to give you for it. But if you don't step up and trade away your "one red paperclip", then there ain't nuthin' that's never gonna happen to that silly little "red paperclip" sitting on your desk – except that maybe it'll get the honour and dignity of holding together your prized stack of baseball cards, including Dan Gladden, Oil Can Boyd, Atlee Hammaker and Rance Mulliniks. It didn't take long with this project to realize I can trade up to a house and help people out – so that's exactly what I'm going to do. I'm more than blown away by the sheer number of people around the world who follow one red paperclip every day. I think there's a lot of people out there that check the site more than I do. The experiences have been awesome, but the most important thing is everyone around here has been awesome. Early on I introduced a self-made word called funtential. ORP has met and exceeded its potential for funtential, but I still think the best is yet to come. Back in the days of one instant party, I came up with another word: "furiousity". Maybe we can say that furiousity is a rare combination of anger/shock/curiousity/inexplicable mindblowingness, and that it really only truly ever occurred for the first time in the history of the world, ever, when I traded the afternoon with Alice Cooper for a KISS snow globe. Yeah, I think that'll probably work just fine as far as the definition of furiousity goes. Anyhow, I'm doing nothing short of trading up to the house in the fastest and bestest way that I feel sticks to my principle of funtential, and I will not stop making trades until I own a house outright. One red paperclip is about the journey and experiences of trading from one red paperclip to a house, and above all else, it's about meeting people along the way. One red paperclip is not a preconceived idea, it has unfolded over the past 10 months and taken on a life of its own. There are no rules. I'm literally flying by the seat of my pants on this. This project is 100% legit and happens in real time. I got the call from Yahk after I randomly said their town's name on the air, and I never could have guessed that I'd ever be on stage with Alice Cooper. Those two serendipitous events totally blew me away by their awesomeness. I have literally no idea what will be offered for my next item or who it will come from. There is no plan, and that's the only plan I've got. I'll announce who I'm trading the snow globe with on Friday June 2nd at 8:18 AM EST. If you want to trade something for whatever my next trade item happens to be, well, you know what to do. Have fun.

Kyle

And the comments rolled in.

Go for the movie role!
Anonymous

CORBIN BERNSEN HAS ONE OF THE LARGEST COLLECTION OF SNOW GLOBES IN THE WORLD. I KNEW THERE WOULD BE A FANATIC OUT THERE. TAKE THE MOVIE ROLE MAN.
Anonymous

Dude, I think Corbin Bernsen just bailed you out (either that or you knew exactly what you were doing all along). (Oh and Corbin, I am a talented videographer in need of a job in the movies :). Have your people call my ... uh ... phone number :)
Adam

My Dad is an antique dealer and he once told me one man's junk is another man's treasure. I think Kyle understands the concept better than my Papa.
Anonymous

Corbin had offered me the movie role when I had the recording contract. More than a month previous. Back then, I'd read his email, but his name didn't ring a bell. My initial reaction was that he wasn't a movie star but just called himself a movie star to get my attention, unlike, of course, the offer from massive KISS fan and world renowned Retired Movie Star Dave Leroux, with his much-heralded performances in film sequels involving animals playing sports.

At the time, I'd called a few people and asked if they knew who Corbin Bernsen was. Unlike me, *everyone* knew who Corbin

Bernsen was. People were excited. They said things like *You got an offer from Corbin Bernsen?!!!* and *The guy from* Major League *and* L.A. Law*!*

I couldn't be as excited, because I'd never heard of Corbin Bernsen before. But whether he was famous or not didn't matter: his offer was great. Like mega great.

A paid, speaking, credited role in a movie.

It was like the recording contract on steroids.

I had called Corbin. He'd answered right away and we talked for a while. We agreed that if I were to accept his offer it had to be a fair trade. I couldn't just take his offer as a donation. If I was going to trade with Corbin, I had to find something he could *actually use*. It had to be a win-win. At the time, I'd just traded the cube van for the recording contract. Corbin said, "Now, that truck. I wish I'd heard about your trading when you had that box truck."

"You mean the cube van?" I said.

"Yeah, whatever it's called. I could've used it for my film company. Look, if something comes along you think will be a fair trade, just let me know."

"I will."

And we left it at that.

After the cube van, the year of rent in Phoenix came, and passed. Corbin didn't exactly have a use for half a duplex, in Phoenix.

When the afternoon with Alice Cooper came along I found out Corbin had met Alice Cooper before, and could pretty much call him up at anytime if he wanted to. Besides, I really wanted to trade with an Alice Cooper fan who could benefit from the meeting.

While Dom and I were in Japan, Evian sent me a link to the

Wikipedia entry for Corbin Bernsen. Under "Trivia" it read: *Has one of the largest collections in the world of snow globes, over 6000.* I had a slight chuckle, then shoved the fact into the compartment of my brain reserved for facts like *I don't remember what those plastic things on the end of shoelaces are called but I know there is an episode of* Seinfeld *that could change that*, and Dom and I went out for sushi.

I never thought to find Corbin a snowglobe until Mark called. Until the flashbulb went off in my head. To just about every single person on the planet, a KISS snowglobe was just another snowglobe. But for Corbin, the renegade snowglobe fanatic, it was like a dream come true. It wasn't just a KISS snowglobe, it was *the* KISS snowglobe.

When I found out Mark had a KISS snowglobe, I called Corbin to see if he was interested. I described all the features of the incredible variable-speed illuminating globe and sent him a picture.

Corbin got back to me and said, "Not only do I want it, I *need* it!"

"So we have a deal then?" I said.

"You bet," he said.

I kept the deal with Corbin secret for a full week. Sure, it was a bit cruel, but no more cruel than an Alice Cooper concert. Actually, it was a lot less cruel than an Alice Cooper concert. Even with all the fury in the blog comments, I didn't spill a single drop of blood. Not one.

The comments made it strikingly apparent the degree to which some people were following my trades. I was amazed how upset people were that I'd "thrown it all away". Of course, I had insider next-trade information and was confident that it would all work out. The comments about the dollar value of the KISS snowglobe made me think about how the value of everything is relative. Something is worth only what somebody else will give you for it. And if you don't trade something for money, you can never attach monetary value to that thing.

Sure, it was unlikely that someone other than Corbin would be so obsessed with snowglobes that he'd make an offer better than a paid speaking role in a movie, but if someone had, I would've leapfrogged Corbin and made the trade with that person. It's not like Corbin and I had a predetermined ironclad agreement or anything. We didn't finalize the deal until after I'd spoken to Mark. And any trade offer for the KISS snowglobe was a legitimate offer. Actually, just between you and me, I was curious to see if somebody would outdo Corbin's offer. But don't tell Corbin that. It'll be our little secret.

Look at the fringes. You never know what you might find. If you look only at the obvious, you'll never see everything else. And there's a whole lot of everything else. Everything else is a *lot* of stuff. You might find something in the sidebars that's more interesting to you than what you saw before. It's all there. There are sentences with six words. Sentences with four words. And sometimes, if you're really lucky, you'll find sentences with nineteen words and an extra period at the end..

Sometimes you need to step backward to take a step forward. I've got a pretty good sense of direction. I hardly ever get lost. But I rarely know the details about where I want to go. I usually just have a rough idea. Sometimes I'll turn off a highway and end up in an unfamiliar place. I usually have a sense of where the highway is and will continue in that direction until I see the highway again and get back on. Once in a while I'll get lost and then find a road that will take me close enough so I can see the highway but I'll be at the end of a road but with no easy way to get back on. The highway might be in sight, but there's no way to reach it unless I floor it and go across a field. So I turn back and look for another way to get to the highway. And find one. Keep an eye on where you want to go, but don't be afraid to step back and find another way to move forward. You can't *always* drive through a field to get back on the highway. Even if you want to. Or have before. Or will again.

one movie role

For an entire week I crossed my fingers and hoped Corbin Bernsen would not die. It's not like I ever *wanted* Corbin Bernsen to die, but never in my life did I have such concern for the man. We're only human. We can go at any moment. Even Corbin Bernsen.

The plane touched down at LAX. As soon as we turned off the runway everyone on the plane feverishly turned on their cell phones and checked messages. I looked over at Dom and we started to laugh. We thought it was funny how people panicked to get back "in touch". As if an extra minute or two mattered. I pulled out my phone at a frantic pace, turned it on and mock-rushed to check messages.

"No messages, whew!" I said and wiped my brow.

We laughed.

Then the horse whinnied. Other passengers looked in my direction and shook their heads. Dom laughed.

"Hello?" I answered meekly.

"Hey, is this Kyle MacDonald?" said a female voice.

"Yep," I said quietly.

"My name is Susan. I'm with CTV television. You're in Los Angeles now, eh?"

"Uh, yeah. We just touched down. How d'you know?" I said.

Apparently Canadian Television was stalking me.

"You posted on your blog that you'd be in L.A. this afternoon," she said.

"Oh, right."

Apparently Canadian Television was *sort of* stalking me.

"Hey listen, can we cover your trade with Corbin Bernsen today?" she said.

I thought about it for a second. How was it possible that a major TV network didn't have a more spectacular story to cover in Southern California? Red carpet event? Slow-speed police chase? Brushfire? This was *Hollywood*. It must've been the slowest news day of the decade. I figured I'd better capitalize on it.

"Yeah, sure. Let me give you the address," I gave her the scoop on where the deal was about to go down, a non-descript warehouse in Van Nuys. The preferable place to trade a snowglobe.

We arrived at Corbin's warehouse/office in Van Nuys. Jody Gnant was in L.A. working on some music, so she joined us for the trade. I pulled the rental car into the parking lot, and looked over at Dom and said, "Ready?"

Dom looked over and said, "*Mais oui*!" She could tell I was nervous. She smiled and said, "Somebody's getting excited about his big trade!"

I didn't know what to say. I just smiled. I grabbed the KISS snowglobe and we walked inside. There he was. Corbin sat below a poster for the movie *Major League*, a huge grin across his face. He stood up and said, "Dude! How's it going?"

I put the snowglobe down and shook his hand. Dom and Jody did as well. But they got hugs too.

Corbin had an amazing office. In one room was a movie theatre. In another was a conference table. In every room were snowglobes.

I handed Corbin the KISS snowglobe box and said, "Here's the snowglobe."

He looked at the box, laughed and said, "Nice! Hey, I even have something to represent my half of the trade."

I perked up my eyebrows and watched as he pulled a stack of papers from his desk. He showed me the front of them. It was the script for *Donna on Demand.*

"Nice," I said.

"It's not finished yet. I hope that's okay. It's all I have so far."

"Sounds good to me!" I said.

We shook hands to seal the deal. Corbin and I stood in front of the *Major League* poster and smiled nicely for Dom's camera.

It was official. I now had a role in a movie. It was the first trade I'd made with a former host of *Saturday Night Live*, so that was cool. I liked the idea that the script for *Donna on Demand* wasn't finished yet. There was so much more to come. The movie script represented an opportunity for somebody.

Corbin pulled the KISS snowglobe from its box and gazed into the glitter. He just gazed at it and said, "Wow."

He plugged it in and flicked the switch. Its insides swirled slowly and changed colours. I showed him the variable speed dial and we watched in wonder as the glitter swirled faster. Corbin just stared and said, "It's like Christmas morning. I've been collecting these for years, and before you tipped me off, I'd never heard about the KISS snowglobe."

He was literally transfixed by the snowglobe.

We looked at him, and shrugged. All of us. Corbin gazed at the snowglobe a moment longer, smiled, and said, "Hey, do you want to see the rest of my snowglobes?"

"*Do we*?!" Dom said.

"Why do you think we came all the way out here?" Jody said.

"Like they said," I said.

"Follow me!" Corbin said.

We walked across the parking lot to a storage unit. Corbin unlocked the door and swung it open. We entered. The unit was filled to the brim with snowglobes. There were more than six thousand of them in the room. We were taken aback. It was amazing. On shelving units were sorted sections of thousands of snowglobes. Christmas snowglobes. Halloween snowglobes. Snowglobes from Europe. Snowglobes, snowglobes, snowglobes.

Corbin gave us a tour, pointing out some of his favourites. In addition to the ones on the shelves, he had plastic bins filled with several hundred duplicates.

"Those are the ones I trade at shows, I'm trying to get rid of most of my duplicate ones," he said.

We walked around for a few minutes, mouths open in wonder at the little worlds inside the plastic and glass domes and globes.

I pointed to a massive shelving unit along one wall filled to the ceiling with green plastic storage bins and said, "Hey Corbin, what's in these big green plastic storage bins?"

He smiled, made a horizontal panning motion with his arm at the expanse of green plastic bins, and said, "Every single T-shirt I've ever worn."

Our jaws dropped as we sized up the bins. There were dozens of them. He flipped one open. It was crammed with T-shirts. At least a hundred in a single bin. He wasn't joking. He literally had every single T-shirt he'd ever worn. In big green plastic bins.

I stood in the middle of the more than six thousand snowglobes and every single T-shirt Corbin Bernsen had ever worn and completely zoned out. It was one of those times when you start to consciously think about breathing and then you can't concentrate on anything else except inhale. Exhale, inhale, exhale. And five minutes go by before you realize you've spent the last five minutes thinking about something to which you normally pay no mind. Inhale, exhale, inhale, exhale. I wasn't there. Normally, I'm hyper-easily amused. A supermarket for me is like Willy Wonka's chocolate factory. *All those different labels. So much to see*. And here I was in Willy Wonka's secret snowglobe lair and all I could think about was breathing. I looked around at all those snowglobes and felt peaceful. I'm not sure if it was the childish simplicity of all the snowglobes, or the amazement of being in the same room as six thousand snowglobes and every single T-shirt ever worn by a middle-aged man.

I just felt at peace with myself. It was bizarre.

Inhale. Exhale. Inhale. Exhale.

We walked outside. I turned and I asked Corbin, "Does anybody have *more* snowglobes than you?"

Corbin said, "Well, there's a bit of discussion about who has the *best* snowglobe collection. There's a guy in France who supposedly has harder-to-find snowglobes than mine, but for sheer numbers, I'm arguably one of the biggest snowglobe collectors in the world."

I made a mental note of Corbin's arguable world snowglobe ranking. Dom, Jody and I said goodbye to Corbin, promised to keep in touch, and went on our way. The CTV film crew that had been following us the entire time turned off the red light on their news-gathering camera.

That night, I found my mental note about Corbin's world ranking, and set out to do something about it. I used the argument that if *many* snowglobes equalled a good collector, then *more than many* snowglobes equalled a great collector. Corbin already had in excess of six thousand, but I was sure his collection would only strengthen if some more came his way. I made a blog post to make my intentions public: I wanted to help Corbin Bernsen become the greatest snowglobe collector the world had ever known. Bar none. If nothing else, just to settle the argument. I love to settle an argument.

Here's an updated version of the blog post. This offer is still valid. Really. Please feel free to join!

JOIN THE CORBIN BERNSEN KISS SNOWGLOBE ARMY!

Do you like to settle arguments? Do you want to make a trade with Corbin Bernsen? You do?! Perfect. To get an autographed picture of Corbin Bernsen and *the* KISS snowglobe, simply send a snowglobe to:

The Corbin Bernsen KISS Snow Globe Army
WORLD HEADQUARTERS:
3940 Laurel Canyon Blvd.
Studio City, California
Box 328
91604
USA

For every snowglobe that Corbin receives, he will mail one proof of membership to the Corbin Bernsen KISS Snow Globe Army. (An autographed picture) The more snowglobes you send, the more highly collectible copies of the identical autographed picture you'll get in return. There's no limit to the number of snowglobes you can send to Corbin, and no limit to the number of autographed pictures you can get in return. The only way you can get one is if you send in a snowglobe to the address above. This offer is opened ended and will never expire! So that's it – what are you waiting for? Join the Corbin Bernsen KISS Snow Globe Army (CBKISSSGA) and get a FREE autographed picture.

Once again, this offer is valid. Yes, today. No, it didn't expire. Please send your snowglobes to Corbin Bernsen to get your autographed picture of him and me and the KISS snowglobe! Let's settle that argument!

With my good deed done for the day, I checked my email. The offers for the movie role were rolling in like gangbusters.

*****Hi Kyle,
I'm the Director of Marketing for GoldTeeth.com and would be willing to trade you a set of 6, 14kt removable gold teeth/grillz in exchange for a role in the movie. These teeth would be custom-made to fit the mouth of whoever traded for them.
Thanks, Scott

*****Hey Kyle!!
I just want to say what your doing is amazing. I dont have much to offer as I'm only 12 but I would love to contribute (and get a movie role). I am willing to give up ALL of my soft toys and believe you me I have a hell of alot of them. Along with that I will give you all of my toys, EVEN CHRISTMAS AND BIRTHDAY presents. I have a loft on the top of my bedroom that is fill to the brim with soft toys. I mean who doesn't love soft toys and just plain games. You could get more than a movie role for my collection of soft toys etc ... I know I'm not offering gold teeth or anything. But I am offering my life's worth of games and soft toys, EVERYTHING!! So please consider my offer. It would mean alot to me to be part of this!!

*****Hi Kyle,
My name is Garrett Johnson and I have been following your trading for awhile now and you have something I'd like to trade for. I

know you are wanting a house and I'm sorry to say I don't have that to offer but I do have some land that you could build on. Before I give you the details I would like to tell you a little bit about myself and why I'm interested in trading. I am a fifty year old auto worker with 32 years on the job and I am close to retiring. I have always been interested in acting but it was an unfulfilled dream. My senior year in High School I received the Drama award and had the male lead in our senior play. I also appeared in several public plays back then to raise money for our town's centennial. I never got the chance to follow up on acting. I moved to Kansas City in 1973 and started working for General Motors and have been there ever since. I have a daughter who is 12 and has been taking acting lessons for a few years so I get to relive a little through her. This is what I have to offer for trade. I own a lot near Warsaw, Missouri at a place called Bent Tree Harbor. It is near Truman Lake but not on the water. I purchased the property in 1984 for about $4100. I am not sure of its current value. The lot is undeveloped and pie shaped. The deed is clear with no back taxes. The dimensions are approx. 66ft across the front, 150ft deep, and 274 feet across the back. I had to ask the count to send me a copy of the survey and don't have it on hand but will let you know the exact dimensions when I receive it. What ever you decide to trade for I want to thank you for the opportunity to chase an old dream I thought had died.

*****I have a Full Blooded Black Female Pug ... She is about 4 months old. I would be willing to trade her for a role in the movie.

*****Hi,

I would like to make you an offer for your Movie Role. I have about 300 Red Bricks. They have been in my driveway for about three

weeks from an old patio I had. Just think of all the things you can do with the bricks. You can stack them in a pyramid. You can make another patio, or you can build a little fortress. The possibilities are endless. I hope you consider my offer.
Thanks. Joe

*****For the movie role, I am making the offer of a lifetime! I have in my posession a winning lottery ticket. The fun part is, I will not reveal the value of the ticket. I WILL guarantee that it is a winner! It is an Indiana scratch-off ticket. I will send it in a security envelope, so as not to reveal the value. This can be fun, and add a little mystery to your quest.
Good Luck, Alexisycho

*****My wife and I are expecting a child in January of next year. We don't yet know if it's a boy or girl, but we are willing to let you name the kid in exchange for the movie role. He/she will still have to have our last name, but other than that you can name them. You can name them after yourself, after your favourite movie star, whatever you want. I will probably shoot down any graphic or explicit names, but other than that it's up to you! Thanks!
Matt and Hannah

*****Hi!
I would like to be in your movie ;) I would like to trade a movie role for a antiques of Iosif Stalin. Do you know who is it? This thing was made in 1933 year, has a long story. It is very old, important and seldom thing. I'm Kate, from Russia, now I live in Ussuriisk, near Vladivostok, may be you hear about it. People from Russia knows about your trade journey, it's very unusually :) Thanks and good luck!

*****Hi!
Yes, I would like to be in your movie. I would like to trade a movie role for a kiss! That's it!
Sincerely, Anna

*****Hi Kyle.
I offer for trade a herd of eight, absolutely gorgeous cattle. My girls come running when they're called and can be scratched and petted. Some are already in calf to the handsome young bull next door :))) They are awesome mothers too. I would love the fun of acting in a movie and the trip would be a bonus too! And besides, I thought it was time Australia got in on this [:)))) The cattle are at Toowoomba Qld, inland by 90 mins or so from Brisbane. The cows are excellent foster mums, very gentle and good natured. There's a couple of heifers in calf (I hope) and a couple of calves, and the three foster mums are due to go into calf again now. People would say I have dramatic leanings but to be honest I am simply throwing this in the ring, just for the fun of it, to see where life takes me. I am a wife and mother of 4 aged from 10 to 18, and so it's been a while since I've done anything impulsive or adventurous, and that mischievous part of me longs for that. It would be such a fun experience! I have some recent stage and public speaking experience and consider myself outgoing and confident. However I also have one young friend who is an aspiring actor, who would grab this opportunity with both hands (and teeth) and RUN with it! Attached a photo of our Murray Grey X foster mum, with newborn back in January this year.
Kerrie.

*****Hi Kyle, I will trade six months of dog grooming for your movie role. Any size, and any breed.
Steph

*****I will offer you one blue paperclip.
Anonymous

And there were hundreds more. The role in the movie played into the same element as the recording contract. People literally offered their souls, body parts, and virginity, for a chance to be in a movie. I was open-minded to most trade offers, but I had to draw the line somewhere. And somewhere was at souls, body parts, and virginity.

This time, people read my earlier blog post about Mark having been in the right place at the right time and picked up the phone. Now everyone wanted to be in the right place at the right time. All the time. Our hotel room in Hollywood was filled with the sound of beautiful horses. The offers were great, and I spoke to people on the phone who were very eager to be involved. But once again, I had to make a tough decision. The emails rolled in incessantly. I wasn't sure what to do. So I just went to bed and put it off until tomorrow.

Everything would sort itself out tomorrow, I was sure.

The next day, Dom and I walked alongside our friend Nirvan on a viaduct in downtown L.A. The sun shone high above. Mr Ed came to life. I flipped him open and said, "Hello?"

"Hello, is Kyle there?" said a man.

"Speaking."

"Hi, Kyle, my name is Bert Roach."

"Hi, Bert, how you doing?" I said.

"Great! And you?"

"Not bad, not bad at all."

"That's good to hear. I'm calling you all the way from the town of Kipling, Saskatchewan," he said.

"Right on, how's Kipling these days?" I said.

"Great! Have you been to Kipling before?"

"Um, no," I said.

"But you've heard of Kipling before?" said Bert.

"Um, no. I can't say I have. Except for this call."

"Oh. Of course! Hey, listen, I'm the community development officer here in town. We've been throwing some ideas around, and would like to make you an offer for the movie role!"

"Cool! What's your offer?" I asked, and squinted as I listened to him.

As I listened, I closed my eyes and turned my face up towards the sun. It was warm. It hit my eyelids and made everything red-orange. Bert's words painted a picture in my mind. A vivid picture. The future. I finished the call and put my silver wild mustang phone back in my pocket. I brought my head back down, opened my eyes, looked forward, and began to smile.

"What are you smiling about?" said Dom.

"Lets walk and talk. I'll tell you everything," I said.

I brought my right foot forward, and we began to walk.

Buy low, sell high, but don't get addicted to the drugs.
This line is funny because I took the common quote "Buy low, sell high" and added the part about "don't get addicted to the drugs" to make you think about high in a different light. High as in intoxicated instead of high as in high value. *That's* why it's funny.

What's your "if"?
Your *if* is a seed of thought that can lead to a reality. An idea. A vision. A potential reality. But in order to make your if come to life you must do something. If your if is to eat a delicious breakfast cereal, then plant a wheat seed and take care of the wheat as it pokes through the soil and grows into a full-grown and *very* delicious Kellogg's Mini Wheat. If your if is to become the greatest snowglobe collector the world has ever known, then start collecting snowglobes. And if your if is to find out what I traded next, then turn the ...

page

Sorry. Had to do it.

Well, now that I've broken the flow, I might as well take this opportunity to mention that Alice Cooper *did* honour his promise of an afternoon with him. Even after I traded him to Mark for a KISS snowglobe. Mark went up to Columbus, Ohio, and snapped this picture. He told me they had a great time.

one house in Kipling

"Really? They offered you a house for the movie role?" said Dom and Nirvan together.

"Well, not exactly. Not yet. But they might. I don't want to jump to conclusions," I said. "That was Bert Roach on the phone. He's the community development officer for the town of Kipling, Saskatchewan. He made me an amazing offer. A piece of land in town, mayor for the day, honorary citizen for life, and get this, they want to build the world's largest red paperclip!"

"Nice," said Nirvan.

"It's like the best offer ever, but I told Bert I wasn't sure I could do it," I said.

"Why not?" said Dom.

"It just didn't feel right to become an honorary citizen for life, and then retrade all that stuff and not actually live there. I told Bert if I were to become an honorary citizen for life, I could only do it with a clear conscience if we lived in town."

"But the town lot?" said Nirvan.

"I guess we could build a house on the land. Or, we could live in a tent!" I said half-jokingly, and looked at Dom with hope in my eyes. She gave me a "look" that told me which side of the half-joke I should act upon. Besides, a tent was a loophole. A tent was temporary. But what about a yurt? Those were permanent … ish. Yes, maybe we could build a yurt. Saskatchewan has a very similar climate to central Asia. Yes, a yurt might just be the ticket. Dom broke my "concentration" and said, "Will they give the movie role to somebody in town?"

"Bert said they want to hold auditions in Kipling for the movie role," I said.

"That's pretty neat," said Dom.

"Yep," I said. "I'm not sure how it's all going to work out, but I've got a good feeling about this."

"Me too," said Dom.

"Me three," said Nirvan.

I held Dom's hand. We walked across the viaduct in the sun.

Over the next week or so, I spoke to Bert many times. During our conversations, I learned how his niece Mary had tipped him off about my attempt to trade from a red paperclip to a house. At a family barbecue, she'd told Uncle Bert all about it. And Uncle Bert, being Kipling's community development officer, was struck with an idea.

And he and I were making that idea a reality.

I sat in our apartment in Montreal and listened to Bert. He wanted to find a way for the trade to work. There had to be a way. He said a sod house could be built on the land. A real, bona fide sod house.

"Dom, what do you think about the idea of living in a sod house?" I said.

"What is that, a *sod* house?" she said.

"A dirt house," I said.

Dom made some sort of noise I can't accurately put in words followed by the lookiest "look" of all time. So the sod house was out. But it was a good idea. I related Dom's sod house "look" to Bert over the phone. He said her look probably meshed with town insurance and building permit policies. Apparently, cave-ins weren't exactly the type of thing people liked to insure nowadays.

Bert said the town of Kipling owned several houses and was about to acquire others for unpaid property taxes, municipal acquisitions, and the like. For the town to trade a house for the movie role, Bert had to convince the town council of the idea and get some official paperwork signed by the land titles division of the provincial government. The process could take weeks.

I told Bert I really wanted to make a trade with Kipling. It felt right. But in order for a trade to take place, it had to be an official offer. Something we could shake hands on. As much as I wanted to be easygoing and serendipitous about everything, I shifted into "negotiator/motivator" mode. I told Bert about the dozens of offers I'd received for the movie role and how more arrived every day. I promised him that a house in Kipling was the best offer, the type of offer I couldn't refuse. I told him about the approaching deadline for me to trade to a house. The July 12 "deadline" I was publicly saddled with because of Patrick Lagacé's article in *Le Journal de Montreal* eight months previous. It was already the end of June. July 12 was not far away. I had only a few weeks to trade up to a house. There's something about being publicly held to your word, whether or not it was actually *your* word. It makes things happen.

Bert said, "I really want to make this happen. I'll see what I can do."

What struck me most about Bert was how he approached the situation with a level head. I was also sure he had a slightly *unlevel* head, in the positive sense, of course. Your head couldn't be too level if you planned to persuade a town council to trade a community asset for a role in a movie. But Bert and I placed value in things that were hard to quantify.

And that's why it was special.

One week later the phone rang. It was Bert. We exchanged pleasantries. He cleared his throat in a very formal way – an old-fashioned, get-down-to-business throat clearing that suggested he had something important to say. And here's what he said:

"Kyle, the Town of Kipling, Saskatchewan, wants you to complete your quest for a house. The Mayor and Town Council, with the support of the employees and residents of the Town of Kipling, have a revised offer for you. We know you will say yes!

"As a new resident to our community you will receive a community welcome package containing local information and promotions from local businesses. The Kipling Chamber of Commerce will give you $200 in Kipling cash. This cash can be spent at any local Chamber of Commerce business. You will be given a key to the town of Kipling. You will become honorary mayor of Kipling for one day. You will be named an honorary lifelong citizen of the town of Kipling. The day we make the trade will be decreed One Red Paperclip Day by our town council, and everyone will be encouraged to wear a red paperclip in honour of your achievements. We will build the world's largest red paperclip in dedication to you and your 'one red paperclip project'.

"Most importantly, to allow you to complete your quest ... we will trade to you a house. The house was built in the 1920s and has been recently renovated. It is located at 503 Main Street Kipling, Saskatchewan, Canada. It is approximately eleven hundred square feet on two floors. There are three bedrooms, one and a half bathrooms, kitchen, living room and dining room. It has white vinyl siding, a new roof and eave troughs that have been put on in the last few years.

We will be sending you pictures of the house as soon as we have had time to touch up the paint.

"We would also like to tell you what we want to do with the movie role. We will hold auditions in Kipling at our local community centre. Auditions will be *Canadian/American Idol* style, with you being the lead judge on the panel. We would also invite Corbin Bernsen and the producers of the movie to be on the panel. Anyone wanting to audition would have to make a donation of some kind, either money or an item of their choice. These items would then be split between the Kipling and District Parks and Recreation and the charity of your choice. We will not take live animals, children, souls, or rain cheques since we have had lots of rain lately."

Bert paused dramatically. Thoughts raced through my mind at warp speed.

The house was located at 503 Main Street? I'd never lived on Main Street before. Any Main Street. And I've shaken Al Roker's hand before. And what about the rest of the offer? Key to the town? Mayor for the day? The world's largest red paperclip? Did I just trade from one red paperclip to a house? Should I pinch myself to see if this is real? No, not yet. I still need to shake hands with Pat, the mayor, for it to be official. I'll pinch myself then. Maybe.

Bert's dramatic pause ended. He had one more thing to say.

"Kyle MacDonald, do you accept our offer of one house in Kipling for one role in Corbin Bernsen's movie *Donna on Demand*?"

If you read the title of this chapter, I'm sure you can imagine what I said.

After nearly a year of constantly looking for a trade, I could kick back with the satisfaction that after fourteen trades with people from all over North America, one red paperclip had just become a house.

As much as I wanted to let everyone know right away, I wanted to let the local newspaper in Kipling, *The Citizen*, be the first to break the story. *The Citizen* hit newsstands once a week. Fridays. It was printed on Wednesdays. Today. Bert called to say that Mike Kearns, the head reporter for *The Citizen*, had called the printer and pleaded with them to stop the press so they could insert the news about the final trade.

For two days I painstakingly denied rumours and pretended I didn't know anything about a house in Kipling being traded for a movie role. Nope, nothing like that at all.

After I learned that *The Citizen* had hit the newsstands in Kipling, I wrote a sparse blog post titled "Interesting".

Just reading the news today. Came across something pretty interesting. Some press-stopping news about a cat being let out of a bag. Huh. Do you think their source is reliable?

The word *cat* was linked to a web page with the front page of the Kipling's weekly newspaper, *The Citizen*, and *bag* took people to the continued article on page two.

Your Community Newspaper!

$1

The Citizen

Kipling, Saskatchewan — Friday, July 7, 2006 — Volume 70, Number 37

It's a done deal!

Kipling High School graduates honoured

Windthorst celebrates Centennial next weekend

Junior Drama Night held at Kennedy

So there it was. Major news networks all over the world called to get the scoop BBC, CBC, CNN, ABC – you name it. But only one news outlet had the world exclusive: *The Kipling Citizen.*

IT'S A DONE DEAL!

It's official! Kyle MacDonald's quest to trade one red paper clip for a house will be fulfilled at Kipling. As reported in earlier editions, Kyle, who for now calls Montreal home, began by swapping a red paperclip for a fish pen; the pen for a doorknob; the doorknob for a camping stove, and so on, and most recently has been offering a speaking role in an upcoming movie, "Donna On Demand". Wednesday, Kipling's community development officer, Bert Roach, along with Mayor Pat Jackson, sweetened the Town's earlier offer during a telephone conversation with Kyle. The original proposal had included a Key to the Town, a day as Honorary Mayor, honorary lifetime citizenship, declaration of One Red Paperclip Day and construction of the world's largest red paperclip in his honour, a community welcome package for him as the Town's newest resident and $200 in Kipling Kash, along with a residential lot. Wednesday, a house was thrown into the mix. With the mayor and some Town staff looking on, and with a CBC television camera rolling at the Town Office, Roach popped the question that promises to set off a sequence of exciting events, both for Kyle and for residents of Kipling: "Kyle MacDonald, do you accept our offer …?" His answer was an unequivocal, "Yes". And amidst applause from those gathered to witness the event, he continued, "This is going to be awesome! That's all I can say!" It is hoped the final "exchange" in Kyle's quest will happen next Wednesday, July 12, a year to the day after it all began. Provided that scheduling arrangements can be made which may involve accommodating international media representatives, Kyle and his girlfriend, Dominique, will become Kipling's newest citizens and proud owners of the house at 503 Main St.

In exchange, the Town will receive rights to a role in an upcoming Corbin Bernsen movie. One facet of the plan is to conduct auditions in Kipling for the part, perhaps as early as September. MacDonald said he has discussed the idea with Bernsen, who has indicated great interest in the concept. MacDonald even hinted that the movie star and his family might become involved in the auditions and accompanying celebrations in some capacity. "This is going to launch a cascading series of events that will turn (yours and my) lives upside down," MacDonald predicted to Roach. He has coined a phrase "Funtential", to describe his journey up to now and the fun which he fully expects is yet to come. While perhaps not a "rags to riches" story, it is certainly one which has attracted widespread attention. oneredpaperclip.com has received more than three million hits since it appeared on the worldwide web last July 12. Now Kipling hopes to cash in to some degree on MacDonald's entrepreneurial notoriety. "I don't think I could be happier," said Roach after the deal, weeks in the making, was struck. "The potential, or rather, funtential, for this is absolutely unbelievable," he said, citing plans to market the world's biggest red paperclip as a tourist attraction on and off the world wide web. Red Paperclip Day could become an annual party, with residents encouraged to wear red paperclips as a Town symbol. The Town is in the process of designing a new logo which is to include a red paper clip. "It's going to be a lot of fun!" he said. The decision finally made, MacDonald confessed to a strange feeling of relief. He supposed it might be something akin to finishing a marathon. By late 2005, just months into his quest, offers were rolling in to Kyle's website "oneredpaperclip.com" at an astounding pace. News services began to take notice and by the time he traded a generator (for "an instant party" which included a beer keg and a neon Budweiser sign) Kyle had received some measure of fame. But it was when he bartered the party (put up by a New York City man) for a snowmobile offered by a Quebec radio and television talk show host, that the 26-year-old achieved celebrity status. Network news features and guest appearances on talk shows became the order of the day for the young man. A much publicized trade for a trip to Yahk, B.C., set off not only a flurry of publicity, but a series of trades which soon took on a showbiz flavour. These included a recording contract, an afternoon with Alice Cooper and a double-switch for a collectible "KISS" (the band) snowglobe which landed Kyle the movie role and

> ultimately prompted Roach to contact him with Kipling's offer. Mayor Pat Jackson shares the enthusiasm expressed by Roach and MacDonald. "We hear so much negativity on the news these days," she said. "It's nice when something refreshing and positive comes along. We are happy to help with Kyle's quest and eager to welcome him to our town." Wednesday's last-minute negotiations were good-natured and when MacDonald asked if the honorary citizenship part of the offer extended to "Dom" (Dominique) as well as to him, the mayor's immediate reply was "By all means, yes! Of course." Lengths of pipe had been fashioned into a 12-foot-long paper clip shape (and painted red) by Town Foreman Kelly Kish, in anticipation for Wednesday's agreement. Roach was quick to say that the finished product will be much larger and may take quite some time to engineer and manufacture. July 12, 2007 is seen as being a realistic and appropriate date to unveil the world's largest red paper clip, which Roach said will serve as a lasting legacy to the entrepreneurship the Town wants to encourage and to acknowledge MacDonald's quest. The two-storey house in Kipling was built in the 1920s and has undergone renovations in recent years. Roach admits some touchups and yard work are needed before turning the keys over to MacDonald, and a work party is scheduled for Saturday, July 8 to do just that. He is hoping residents will jump on the bandwagon and that there will be lots of help that day, in preparation for welcoming Kyle and Dom to Kipling. Any positive support people can lend to the project is appreciated, he said. To get involved call Bert at XXX-XXXX.

The instant I posted the link to *The Citizen* on my site, the Internet came alive with blog posts and news articles. The Associated Press ran another story, and things went haywire mediawise, as with my pay-phone-hoarding stopover in Philadelphia. But this time, things were even *haywirer*, albeit, with fewer pay phones. Over the following days, a link to www.oneredpaperclip.com was featured on the front pages of the websites Yahoo!, AOL, BBC, CBC, ABC, MSN, CNN and FOX News, and countless others. My picture was even on the front of *Le Journal de Montréal*, holding the giant red paperclip Dom's mom had made!

Within a matter of days, four million people visited www.oneredpaperclip.com. The palomino nearly had a heart attack. Bert and I decided the Labor Day weekend would be the best time to hold the housewarming party. I appeared on dozens of TV and radio shows, including CNN and *Good Morning America*. On live TV I openly invited *everyone* to the housewarming party in Kipling on the Labor Day weekend. By now I was on a first-name basis with dozens of DJs around the world who had called frequently and continually spread the word to their listeners about the current trade item up for grabs. I spoke to Ian and Margery from FM107 for at least the seventh time and encouraged the fine folks of the twin cities to get ready for a big housewarming party up in Kipling. It was easier than sending out invites.

I wrote a blog post about the party:

We have no idea how many people are going to show up. No idea at all. Kipling is home to a shade more than 1100 residents. With Dom and I living there, it'll be a shade more than 1102. There is one motel. It has 25 rooms. I'm pretty sure there'll be more than 25 rooms worth of people who'll show up for "Saskatchewan's Biggest Housewarming Party, Ever". The name demands it. We literally have no idea where everybody's going to sleep. I guess we'll figure it out over the next little while. Bring RV's or something like that – we'll find room for you somewhere. I call dibs on my bed. Actually, Bert told me 503 Main Street isn't furnished, so I guess I don't even have a bed yet. I call dibs on my future bed then. The good news is that there are three grocery stores in town so we probably won't have to worry about running out of food.

The best part was that I'd never even seen what the house looked like when Bert and I made the trade over the phone. I saw an image of it for the first time on *The National* on *CBC* just like everyone else. It was a two-storey square house with three bedrooms and was white with a red trim. If you asked a child to draw you a house, 503 Main Street was what you'd get. It was perfect.

But I still had to shake the mayor's hand for the trade to be official.

Dom and I sat on an airplane while it made the three-hour flight from Montreal to the capital of Saskatchewan, Regina. We met Kipling residents Eldon Gibson and Kelly Kish at the airport, and stayed the night in Regina. My parents met up with us at the hotel, Mom cut my hair, and everyone tried to sleep. It was impossible. I was nervous. And excited.

We awoke and drove toward Kipling. The flat, gently rolling prairie spread in front of us. Green, yellow and blue fields stretched as far as the eye could see. Silos, grain elevators and farmhouses dotted the horizon as we drove east on highway 48. Every so often we'd pass through a town. Each town was like a small island in a sea of endless fields.

At one point, we pulled to the side of the road to get a closer look at a new bulk grain terminal. Eldon and Kelly told us how Kipling was the division split for grain distribution in Canada. The grain from fields east of Kipling was shipped to the east, toward Montreal. The grain from fields west of Kipling was shipped to the west, toward Vancouver. Kipling sat on the continental divide of grain. I wasn't sure if a fact like that was something I should take as a deep and meaningful metaphor about where Dom and I were in our lives, or just as something fun I could think about the next time I did a word search on the back of the box of Mini Wheats. Both, I figured, but really, that would depend on the difficulty of the word search.

We got back in the van and continued to drive east. A short while later, a shiny silver grain elevator came over the horizon. My heart skipped a beat.

The island was in the *distance.*

The *distance* was getting closer.

As we neared the grain elevator and slowed down to the town

speed limit, a large sign came into view. A fifteen-foot-tall "old tyme" scroll of paper sat upright beside a feather pen. On the paper were the words "Kipling Welcomes You".

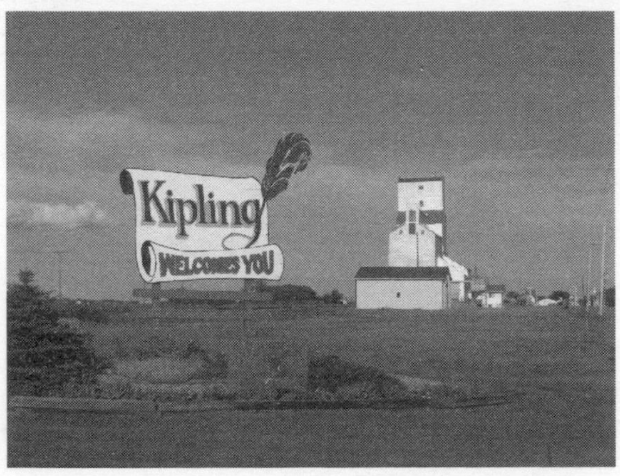

As we drove past the shiny grain elevator, a large "Kipling Co-op" sign on the side of the road read, "Welcome Kyle & Dom".

Kipling's town motto is "Where If Becomes Reality". I realized something. We were the *if.* This was the reality.

We pulled into a parking lot not far from 503 Main Street and nervously got out of the van. Hundreds of people stood across the road. A buzz was in the air. It felt like when Alice Cooper arrived in Alice, North Dakota. But this time it wasn't Alice Cooper who had to remind himself he was *the* Alice Cooper. I had to remind myself I was me. *The* me. I was very nervous. It's one thing to create a website and go on television shows seen by millions of people around the world. It's another thing completely to appear before a crowd of hundreds. In one place.

Dom and I walked through the crowd to the front of the house to meet Bert and Pat and the rest of Kipling, Saskatchewan. We faced the crowd and waved, shyly. Mom took our picture, just like the first trade with Ronnie and Corinna in front of the 7-Eleven.

There's a photograph that's famous in Canada. It was taken on November 7, 1885, just outside the town of Craigellachie, British Columbia. A crowd of onlookers stand around a white-bearded, top-hat-sporting man named Donald Smith as he drops a sledgehammer onto an iron spike, driving it into a piece of wood. The motion had happened countless times before. In countless places. But this spike was different. It was the last spike in the Canadian Pacific Railway, the country's first transcontinental railroad. After years of hard work by many people, the dream was finally realized. A train could now travel across the country, from one ocean to the other. In the photo, dozens of people stand around, fixated on the last spike as it is pounded into the railway tie. The onlookers want to witness the final blow from the sledgehammer, the exact moment the railway is complete. It's one of the most defining moments in Canadian history, a single motion that tied so many people together. I've always been fascinated by this picture. How one motion can hold so much gravity. How a single action can mean so much.

The ceremony at 503 Main Street begins. We stand for the national anthem. Mom and Dad are right behind us. Speeches are made, formal introductions take place.

Pat, the mayor, raises a piece of paper in the air.

"Here in my right hand is the deed to the house behind us. It is my honor to hereby ask Kyle MacDonald to step forward with his trade item and sign this piece of paper to make the trade official." The crowd claps. I step forward. A hush falls over the crowd.

I smile and hand over the movie script. Pat hands me a pen. I sign the deed. We smile.

Pat says, "To make this official, it must be witnessed. Gord, will you?"

Gord, the Mountie, steps forward and signs the deed.

Pat says, "Welcome to Kipling."

We cut a red ribbon with a pair of scissors.

Dom and I hold hands and walk up the stairs. I reach out and open the front door. I face the crowd to speak. My lip starts to tremble.

It is so real.

So perfect.

So silent.

Dom holds my hand.

We say thank you.

We wave to the crowd.

And walk through the door.

Into the future.

Freelance story from the *Brisbane Courier Mail*, July 13, 2006.
Inspired by Success by Ruth Limkin

ONE red paperclip. Fourteen trades. One amazing story. In what must be one of the best feel-good stories of recent days, Kyle MacDonald, of Quebec, Canada, did the improbable by effectively trading one red paperclip for a house.

Yep a house. It's two storeys, recently renovated, and situated at 503 Main St, Kipling, Saskatchewan. (The town is also throwing in a key to the city.)

He did it in only 14 trades and in a year, officially taking possession of the house yesterday.

MacDonald had been renting in Quebec but decided he wanted to own a house. He didn't have enough money for a house, but he did have one red paperclip. MacDonald placed his faith in the concept of relative value – that one person's trash is another person's treasure. So, with a big dream, and a whole lot of determination, he embarked on his quest.

Stories like this are water to the soul. When we're constantly reminded of the problems in this world and the dark and violent side of human nature, stories such as this shine forth and captivate us. MacDonald's blog had more than 3,800,000 hits, as people from around the world heard about the guy who was trading a red paperclip for a house. We want to be a part of great stories. We want to celebrate a win. We want to remind ourselves that wonderful things can happen.

Winston Churchill once said, "The pessimist sees difficulty in every opportunity. The optimist sees the opportunity in every difficulty." And some of us can see a house in a paperclip.

It takes courage to face the challenges life brings us and still dare to dream that we can make a difference. It's easier to throw our hands up and admit defeat, or to point the finger of blame at our parents, our children, the government, or society. And yet we only hurt ourselves by doing so. If we never unleash the passion and determination that enriches life, we end up all the poorer for it.

The attitude we take in our approach to life literally defines our days. For even though we may go through seasons of difficulties, those with a positive attitude will always end up stronger and more resilient.

Could the reason the red paperclip story has captivated so many people be that we resonate with daring greatly? We may have grown weary but we still want to live significant lives. It's here that our celebrated Western individualism has tripped us up.

Thinking we have to go it alone and just be strong, we have forgotten one vital component.

MacDonald could never have got that house without people who were willing to be part of his journey and cheer him on.

Like MacDonald, each of us needs people who can be a source of strength and encouragement. Similarly, we have the privilege of being that for others.

Life's too short to be mean-spirited. Those who encourage others often find that they themselves are bolstered.

A few kind words or a simple act of generosity can be all someone needs to spur them onwards.

We can live passionately and greatly. We need courage to dream big, determination to stay positive and people who will encourage us.

And every so often, we just need to remember how a bloke from Canada turned a red paperclip into a house.

Ruth Limkin, Brisbane, Australia

This article first appeared in the *Brisbane Courier*

Saskatchewan's biggest housewarming party, ever

A few weeks after we walked through the front door of 503 Main Street, and into the future, Kipling hosted Saskatchewan's Biggest Housewarming Party, Ever. And it lived up to its billing. People came from far and wide for the party. Canada, the States, and even Europe. People drove from both coasts and from Kentucky, Kansas and places afar. Since this is a book, I can't really use the expression "words can't describe" to describe the atmosphere in town but if I could, I would. Here's my snapshot of the weekend, in no particular order.

Main Street was closed to traffic. It was transformed from a slab of grey to a slab of life. People brought out homemade pies, cabbage rolls. They baked for days, weeks leading up to the event. Since it was harvest time, balls of hay lined the streets. Cobs of corn were piled high in the back of a pickup truck. Hungarian meals. Meals at the Legion hall. Bouncy castles for the kids. People arrived in cars with backpacks and tents. The campground was filled with people. Stands were set up on Main Street. Chalk murals on the street. Clothes for sale. Local arts and crafts for sale. Nirvan and Levi's stand for *The 1 Second Film*. Everyone did something.

It was amazing to watch and be part of everything. The community and everyone who arrived stepped up and pulled together to create an unforgettable weekend. Bert and his wife,

Marcie, along with countless others, had continually organized things since July 12, and now they came together. There was a massive party at the hockey arena, three nights in a row. Local music acts Brad Johner, Butterfinger and hometown singer Alec Runions. There were Mounties. On horseback. Just like you'd imagine. The Sasktel hot air balloon soared over town. A spectacular fireworks display set against the wispy green background of the northern lights. People dropped off housewarming gifts at the house. The air was full of energy from people.

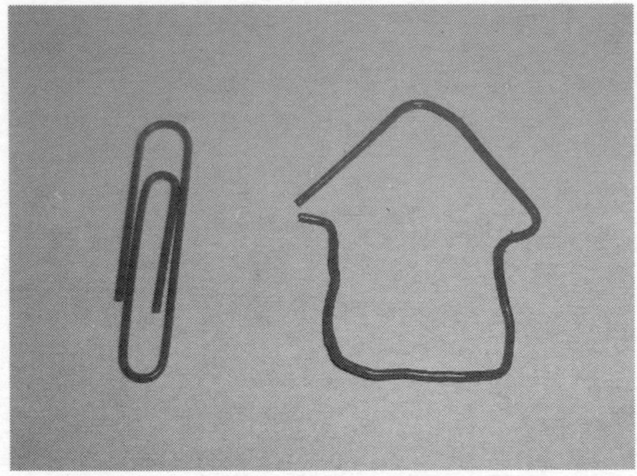

One way to turn a red paperclip into a house.

(From left to right) Mom, Annie, Kyle, Corinna, Mark, Jody, Dad, Shawn.

Being mayor for the day has its privileges.

Kipling resident Ed Clark in front of the crowd on Main Street in Kipling for the housewarming party.

You can't really pay money for a picture like this.

Everyone who thought my idea was crazy. Family. Friends. Friends of friends. New friends. Almost every person I'd traded with was there. Brendan and Jody Gnant took the stage separately, with their bands, and together, as Jody sang her song "Red Paperclip" while every trader present was onstage. Dancing.

Colin Pearson, a family friend from way back, performed a song he'd recently composed about one red paperclip called "I Made a Friend Today".

And we all made many friends during the weekend. At harvest time. Bert called it Saskatchewfun. And it was. It was absolutely massive. I even grew a handlebar mustache for the occasion. In the mornings I sat in our kitchen and shook hands while I ate cereal. It was unbelievable.

Saskatchewan's Biggest Housewarming Party, Ever, was an unrepeatable collaborative experience totally improvised by like-minded folk. It was like we were all "writers" writing our first book. We just did the best we could, figured things out as we went along, and asked for help if needed. Like when I asked Mom to read this chapter and comment:

Mom, "the editor": Describe a bit about the community pulling together in six short weeks to put on this fair … community groups, organized dinners and baked pies, farmers and equipment suppliers showcased their equipment on the street. A chip truck set up shop in the middle of the road. Every business sold T-shirts with "I ❤Kipling". The motel put on a fantastic buffet for the crowds. Everyone was stoked. I was stoked. Dom's mom and sisters and her grandmère flew in. They were stoked. Your parents drove out. Took them three days. They were stoked. Your cousin Carm came with her husband Ricky and their two little boys. All family and friends came. All who could. M

Yes. Like Mom said, she was stoked. I was stoked. Everybody was stoked. That's what the kids are saying these days, right?

Mom said there was "magic in the air". I wasn't exactly ready to use a word like *magic* to describe how it felt, because my friends were around, but I agreed with Mom.

Everyone was there. Family, friends, traders, people from town, people from out of town, people who'd followed the story, and people who just wanted to see what all the fuss was about.

It was a real housewarming.

Our house was very warm.

The entire weekend was like one of those dreams where everyone you know is in one place at the same time. But it was real. I even pinched myself to make sure. Sure enough it felt like a pinch. Nirvan said it was like the end of a *Scooby Doo* episode where everyone comes together to solve the mystery.

In a lot of ways, he was absolutely right. Except for the unmasking-a-villain part.

Every trader who could make it posed for this picture: Kyle, Corinna, Annie, Shawn, Michel, Jeff, Bruno, Jody, Leslie, Mark, Corbin, Pat, Bert.

I could go on endlessly and describe the weekend in further detail until the cows came home. And since we're talking about Kipling, Saskatchewan, there's a pretty good chance a cow might actually come home.

I'll bring it back and finish this story. Or at least give it my best shot.

On Saturday evening, public auditions were held at the community centre for the role in *Donna on Demand.* Hundreds of people packed the hall and watched as more than a dozen people performed roles selected by Corbin. The performances were incredible. An amazing showcase of local talent. But only one person would get the role. And Corbin would announce the winner the following morning, Sunday.

Sunday was the big day. I awoke with a start. I opened my eyes and I stared at the ceiling.

Today is the day. I can feel it.

A crowd began to gather at the end of Main Street, right in front of the house. Bleachers were set up. Bleachers on Main Street. The stage presentation was about to begin. I walked outside.

Yes, now is the time. I know what I want to do, I just don't know how I'm going to get there.

Hundreds, if not thousands, of people stood on Main Street and sung "Oh Canada". Jody sang the Star Spangled Banner. Her rendition was so moving it brought people to tears. The pair of Mounties on horseback were there, a band, dancers, politicians, the whole nine.

Mayor Pat Jackson took to the stage and told a brief story of how it had all happened. She invited me up onstage to proclaim me honorary mayor for the day.

I walked up onstage.

But an important piece of the puzzle is missing. It just won't work. I can't do it. I'll wait and do it another time.

I was proclaimed honorary mayor for the day. Pat handed me the mayoral gavel, which went spectacularly with the wooden key to the town in my left hand and the "Mayor" sash over my shoulder. I thanked her for the honour and walked to the podium. I held the gavel in the air, looked out into the sea of faces, and said "All right, let's clean up this town."

Everyone laughed pretty hard. It had to be said. The situation demanded it. I might never be mayor again.

I laughed and said, "Well, I guess I need to enact some crazy laws by decree, or something." I rambled for a few moments and said things like, "Everyone who has a moustache gets free high fives" – things like that. After I'd drifted well into Ramblesaurus Rex territory, I invited all the traders and Dom to come up onstage. Twelve of the fourteen traders were there: Corinna, Annie, Shawn, Michel, Jeff, Bruno, Brendan, Jody, Leslie, Mark, Corbin, and Bert. They and Dom joined Pat and me onstage. Corinna had the original red paperclip with her. It hung around her neck, safely stored behind glass in a wooden frame. I introduced everyone and told the whole story from the red paperclip right up to the house. I talked about Ricky's shirt and invited him onstage to graciously return it to its original owner. I thanked him, but said it was a bit too big. My version of the story was just like you've read in this book, only it didn't take so long. Unless of course, you're a speed reader, then it probably took longer. It was an amazing scene. Nearly everyone who'd made it happen was in the same place at the same time.

I looked out into the crowd. Almost everyone I know is out there. It's perfect. How can it work? There must be a way. Think. I searched. Nothing. I looked at everyone onstage. *There must be a way.*

I stepped back from the podium, and Corbin came forward to announce the winner of the role in the movie. I turned to all the traders and asked if they could please stay onstage after the winner was announced, as I had one more thing to say. Corbin made a heartfelt speech about how much he was touched by the people of Kipling. He complimented the entire town. It was a great speech. We all felt Corbin's connection with Kipling.

And then I saw it. *It's perfect.* I smiled. *Today is the day.*

Corbin switched into Hollywood showman mode to announce the winner of the movie role. Most of the audience had been at the auditions the night before, and everyone leaned forward with anticipation. Corbin had deliberately worn a dark T-shirt over a white one. The winner's name was written on the white T-shirt, hidden from view.

He said, "And the winner of the movie role is ..."

He spun around and lifted up his black T-shirt. (I wondered if it would end up in his collection.) Confetti cannons at the sides of the stage fired into the air. A roar of applause shot through the crowd.

Written on the back of the T-shirt was the name of the winner: Nolan G. L. Hubbard.

Corbin on stage announcing the winner of the movie role auditions.

For Nolan, nineteen years old and born and bred in Kipling, it was a dream come true. His performance the night before had blown the audience away. Now was his turn to be blown away. He stumbled onto the stage in disbelief. He shook Corbin's hand, thanked him profusely, put on the shirt and approached the lecturn.

Nolan Hubbard after he got the role.

Nolan shook with excitement. The joy on his face was unmistakable. He said, “I’ve wanted to do this my whole life. I can’t believe it.” He turned to Corbin, said thank you again, and turned back to the crowd with a giant smile on his face. It was the perfect moment.

Nolan Hubbard onstage in Kipling during the housewarming party. Just after he was announced recipient of the movie role.

Nolan talked for a few energetic moments, and then walked away from the lecturn.

Now is the time. It's the perfect moment. I know it's right, but I'm afraid.

Dom saw my hesitation. She looked me in the eye and said, "You wanted to say something else?"

"Yes," I said, nervously.

What would I do if I weren't afraid? Eat cheese? Probably. We all would. But what else would I do?

I took a deep breath, and stepped forward. I turned to Corinna, pointed to the red paperclip stored safely inside the picture frame around her neck, and said, "Can I borrow that for a second?"

Corinna nodded and handed it to me.

I looked over at my brother Scott. With a confident smile on his face he gave me a thumbs-up. He knew. I don't know *how* he knew, but he did.

This is it.

I approached the lecturn.

It's perfect. It's, so, real. So . .

My lips quivered and I opened my mouth.

So … now.

Words came from my mouth.

"Five years ago I met Dom in a basement of a hostel in Edmonton. I was on a week off from my job as a roughneck on the oil rigs; she was on her way back to Québec with her sister, Marie-Lou, from a three-month trip in Whistler. I offered them a lift to the Greyhound station, where they were about to board a bus destined for Montreal. They accepted the offer, we hung for a few hours at the hostel, then we packed their bags in my car. I asked a guy named Mark who was hanging out with us if he wanted to come along for the ride. He did. We drove to the bus station, we said our goodbyes to Dom and Marie-Lou, and Mark and I walked back outside toward my car. As we neared the car, Mark looked over at me and said, 'Did you get their phone number or email address?'

'No, why?' I said.

"I'm not the type of guy to ask for phone numbers or anything like that, so I was nervous.

'Why? Why not?' Mark said. 'You never know if you'll go to Québec one day or something. Dominique and Marie-Lou seemed really cool. It'd probably be nice to hang out with them again. And the older one, Dominique, she liked you.'

'Really?' I said.

'Trust me,' he said.

"I walked back inside with my hands in my pockets. I was nervous. I looked down, kicked the ground, and shyly asked if they wanted to swap phone numbers and, you know, stuff. Dom looked up at me with a big smile and said, "*Mais oui*!"

Six months later I was atop an active volcano in Indonesia and met a guy from Québec named Mathieu. I told Mat how I'd kept in touch with Dom and Marie-Lou and said how I wanted to travel to Québec. As Mat and I travelled together for the next few weeks through South-east Asia, he convinced me to come to Québec that summer. At nearly the same time, my brother, back in Canada, emailed and asked if I wanted to tag along in the van he and some friends were about to drive across the country. It was perfect. Everything lined up. I bought a small wooden fish statue on a ferry boat in Indonesia, transported it across Canada on the dashboard of the van, and when we arrived in Dom's village of St-Alexis-des-Monts, I gave it to Dom as a gift. I'd planned to stay with Dom in her village for a few days, but, well, never really left. Dom and I have been together since the day I gave her the wooden fish."

I looked out into the crowd gathered in front of the stage on Main Street in Kipling. There was a hush in the air. Yes, a hush. I took a deep breath. I held the red paperclip up in the air. The original red paperclip I'd traded for the fish pen. The most important trade of all.

I smiled and said, "Even though she never made a trade to get to the house, Dom's as much a part of this journey as everyone else on the stage. She helped out more than I can ever explain. When I became obsessed with trading up to the point where I forgot to do simple things like eat or sleep, Dom was there. If Dom hadn't been there, it would've all just been a dream. And now that we're all here, it's like a dream come true."

I looked over at Dom and bent the paperclip into a loop. A circle.

I twisted the ends together. It was in the shape of a ring.

Everything had come full circle.

I walked toward Dom.

Got down on one knee.

My arm came forward.

I held out the red paperclip.

And looked into her eyes.

PR
MAKING

epilogue:
Grandpa brings it

Steve, (Kyle's buddy since homeroom first year of Junior High): I can't believe you left out the best part! The part about your grandpa!

Kyle: What part about my grandpa?

Steve: You didn't hear what he said?

Kyle: Nope.

Steve: Oh man, it was priceless. Right after Dom said *oui*, and everyone started to cry, and everyone was so happy and emotional and hugged and shook hands at the side of the stage, your grandpa came up onstage and said "I'm Kyle's grandfather, and I'd like to say something." The audience let out a big collective groan, like, *Uh oh, here's Kyle's grandpa. He's gonna ruin the moment and ramble on for ages and make the situation really awkward for everybody.*

Kyle: Did he?

Steve: He said, "I'd just like to say, there's one other person who made all this happen."

Kyle: Who?

Steve: He stood up straight and proud, pointed to himself, and said, "Me."

What's your Kipling?

acknowledgements

First off, before I get deep and sentimental, I'd like to thank Google for allowing me to continually copy/paste hard-to-spell words from your fantastic website into this book. Yes, I did mean *Acknowledgements*. And *Stroumboulopoulos.*

One red paperclip was never about a silly red paperclip or a house at 503 Main Street in Kipling, Saskatchewan. It was about everyone who made it happen. Thanks Corinna, Rhawnie, Annie, Shawn, David, Marcin, Michel, Jeff, Bruno, Brendan, Jody, Leslie, Mark, Corbin, Bert, Pat and everyone from Kipling. I pieced it together, but you made it happen. Give yourself a good pat on the back. We did it.

Alice Cooper, special thanks for spending an "afternoon" with Mark, even after I traded you away for a KISS snowglobe. Thanks to George Stroumboulopoulos, everyone at the *The Hour* and everyone in Yahk who helped find a win-win situation as the result of a blog-based ultimatum/petition about a lie involving hypnosis. We somehow helped turn Yahk into something none of us could ever have imagined. I'm glad I picked Yahk to mess with.

To everyone in Kipling, Saskatchewan, thank you for the unbelievable welcome to town. Dom and I are continually grateful to be part of the community. Kipling truly is the place where *if* becomes reality.

Dan, thanks for helping drive. Are you hungry?

Evan, thanks for being so nice.

Ricky, thanks for letting me borrow the shirt.

Marc, Brandon and everyone who pulled strings to get these words on paper, thanks. It's true: there is no "I" in book.

Mom, Dad, Scott, Grandpa, and all family and friends who deserve a mention but I'm too nervous to start to name names because if I forget to mention you I'll never hear the end of it. Wait a second:

A very special thanks to ________________ for your ________________ and unforgettable ____________. You really are the ____________. P.S. – You have beautiful ________________.

Come find me. Bring a pen. And I don't want to hear anything about loopholes.

To everyone out there who supported the idea, or told me I was nuts: thanks. It all helped.

And to Dom. You made it happen. I just thought it worked itself out.

I hope you enjoyed it, I sure did.

Have fun,

Kyle